# KISSING ASS

the art of office politics

# KISSING ASS

## the art of office politics

Clyde D'Souza

EBURY PRESS

An imprint of Penguin Random House

EBURY PRESS

USA | Canada | UK | Ireland | Australia
New Zealand | India | South Africa | China | Singapore

Ebury Press is part of the Penguin Random House group of companies
whose addresses can be found at global.penguinrandomhouse.com

Published by Penguin Random House India Pvt. Ltd
4th Floor, Capital Tower 1, MG Road,
Gurugram 122 002, Haryana, India

Penguin
Random House
India

First published by Random House India 2012



10 9 8 7 6 5 4 3 2

The views and opinions expressed in this book are the author's own and the facts are as reported by him which have been verified to the extent possible, and the publishers are not in any way liable for the same.

ISBN 9788184002270

Typeset in Bailey Sans ITC by InoSoft Systems, Noida

Printed at Repro India Limited



www.penguin.co.in

FSC
www.fsc.org
MIX
Paper from
responsible sources
FSC® C047271

This is a legitimate digitally printed version of the book and therefore might not have certain extra finishing on the cover.

For

*Amy, my mum,*

*for laughing at my jokes*

*(it's all her fault)*

PHOTO OF ASS

YOUR PHOTO

| THIS BOOK BELONGS TO YOU |
| --- |
| Employee Name: |
| Designation: |
| Company Name: |
| Name of Bastard Boss: |
| Current Salary: |

# Contents

# FOREWORD
# AKA PRAISE FOR THE BOOK

'Compromises were made in sticking to any actual facts and hard research, but this is no lame-duck book, unlike a certain boss that I report to.'

*Minister*

'A revolutionary scam pulled off by the author with great finesse. Will crumble the weak pillars of the entire corporate establishment and result in notional losses.'

*Former telecom minister*

'I denounce this as nothing but impotent drivel attempting to pass off as wisdom. Cleansing rituals of tantric sex would be required for those who read this book. Twitter me @yourSwami.'

*Disgraced godman*

# PRAISE FOR FUTURE BOOKS

'A revolution in Indian writing. Should be made into a movie.'

*Bestselling novelist*

'This is shocking, India!! Whatever the hell am I talking about!'

*Screaming news-anchor*

# INTRODUCTION

## Why Work?

What better way to start this book than by asking that question with which we begin every Monday morning: Why work?

Once upon a non-working time, Homo sapien man had it simple—that is, depending on whether he was pure veg, non-veg, or Jain veg. He worked mostly for food and replaced the neem leaves around his groin every time he soiled them. But the passage of time and no threat from velociraptors led him to invent commerce. This in turn led to credit card complications and working for reasons so far removed from his primary needs it totally fried his brains. As time passed by, the reasons for which we worked became myriad, and, frankly, astonishing.

| What We Worked For | | | | |
|---|---|---|---|---|
| **Food** (also genital coverings and a nice warm cave with broadband) | **Staying Alive** (although we could have just killed the guys who enslaved us) | **Exchanging Things** (first examples of partner swapping) | **Money** (to invest in stocks in order to get more money. We then ate that money and found inner peace) | **Farmville** (to buy virtual vegetables and water our virtual plants. Shit gotta go!) |
| **Sapien Time** | **Slave Era** | **Barter Age** | **Commerce** | **E-age** |
| **Evolution Timeline** | | | | |

(*contd*)

(*contd*)

**History of Jobs in India**

| | **Pre-Independence** | **Independent India** | **Licence Raj** | **Liberalized but Corrupt** | **Emerging Economy (Obama-Certified)** |
|---|---|---|---|---|---|
| Popular Jobs | **1. East India Company** Gainfully—but with a tinge of guilt—employed by colonizers.<br><br>Or | **Government Jobs** Your grandfather worked his entire lifetime in one company. One company, mind you. | **Gulf Jobs** Fishermen Arabs turned into oil sheikhs and they lured Indians with their tax-free economy and duty- | **Call-Centre Employee** While America created FB and Google, we answered calls on their behalf. | **1. IIM-bred Consultants** Gainfully—but with no tinge of guilt—employed by colonizers disguised as corporations. |

(*contd*)

*(contd)*

| | Pre-Independence | Independent India | Licence Raj | Liberalized but Corrupt | Emerging Economy (Obama-Certified) |
|---|---|---|---|---|---|
| | **2. Untouchable** Painfully—but with a tinge of fatalism—employed by one's own race. | Now that's loyalty. Or lack of choice. | free shopping. | | **2. Interns** Same as 'Untouchables' |
| Salary | 1. Enough to accumulate adequate wealth for Parsis | Your grandfather was grateful he had a job that paid him the | Converted into the prevailing exchange rate and | Class 12 dropouts can earn more than their dads. | 1. Refer to latest *TOI* article and fume with jealousy. |

*(contd)*

*(contd)*

| | | | | | |
|---|---|---|---|---|---|
| | to buy vast areas of land. 2. Whatever the dog didn't eat. | same amount year after year. And take your dad screaming and shouting to his native place because the train ticket was paid for. | smuggled into India to build houses in Kerala. | | 2. Your IIM boss will tell you, 'The experience is worth an IIM degree.' And then you spend the weekend working on his presentation. |
| Perks | 1. You got to speak English. And indulge in occasional illicit relationships | Once 'permanent' no one could fire your grandfather | A weird accent, gold chains, and brides who wanted to be | A weird accent, gold credit cards and 'night shift' as an | 1. No accountability. Will tell you who to lay off. |

*(contd)*

(*contd*)

| | **Pre-Independence** | **Independent India** | **Licence Raj** | **Liberalized but Corrupt** | **Emerging Economy (Obama-Certified)** |
|---|---|---|---|---|---|
| | with the gora memsahibs.<br>2. Day off from cleaning shit. | even if he didn't do any work. Most grandfathers came to work to escape their spouses and chill out with their colleagues. | married to an NRI. | excuse for late night drinking | 2. All accountability. First to be laid off. |

<table>
<tr><th colspan="2">Why We Really Work Today</th></tr>
<tr><th>Cool Reasons</th><th>Boring (but real) Reasons</th></tr>
<tr><td>• I am very passionate about this job<br>• I have wanted to do this since I was a kid<br>• I want to excel in this field and exceed all expectations<br>• It gives me a lot of money. Though I don't really know why<br>• I get to wear formal clothes with pointy shoes<br>• Free AC, dude!<br>• Free Internet, man!<br>• I could possibly get laid<br>• Front for my night job as Batman</td><td>• I would have to eat dirt otherwise. I haven't eaten it since I was five<br>• Keeps me from getting bored<br>• We didn't have money so I started working when I was a kid<br>• My father-in-law does not pay my EMIs<br>• It gives me space from my wife/husband<br>• Society accepts me because I 'go to work'<br>• Two weeks ago a kind lady from the credit card company called to remind me about my late payment. Yesterday a very big man came to my door. Ouch!</td></tr>
</table>

## Work-Life Balance

Ever since some genius invented work as a means of earning a livelihood, mankind struggled with attaining a work–life balance. Mostly work won, depending on how much you weighed.

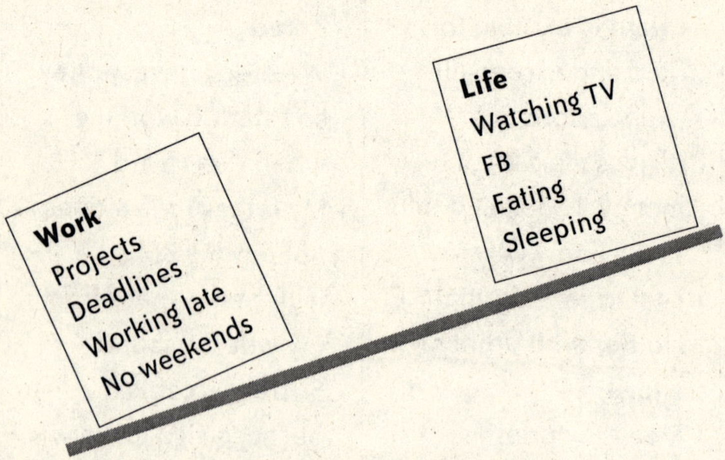


There is no way to correct this imbalance. It's just one of those lifelong conditions we have to live with. Your 9 to 5 battle will be dealt with post-office drinking sessions, bitching sessions, shopping sessions. All of which will lead to credit card bills, which can only be cleared if you work and get paid.

## Quick Quiz

**1. Have you murdered an elderly Parsi couple and stolen their valuables?**

a. Yes
b. No

**2. Can you prove your dad is Ambani, Tata, Tendulkar or, even better, all three?**

a. Yes
b. No

If your answer to the above questions is No then I regret to inform you that you have no option but to work. So stop crying and read on.

## Why Kiss Ass?

Doing your job is only *part of the job.* Politics is part of human nature whether it's in Parliament, the bedroom, or your workstation. Get used to it and get good at it!

Consider this book as your cheater's guide to work, a handy chit that you can refer to when the boss is not looking. Maybe you are a fresher and are wondering what to say at your interview, or perhaps it's a Saturday and your boss is calling you right now (what a bastard, quick, turn to the chapter Email Etiquette), or you want to get a promotion but don't know how.

Whatever it is, this book has been designed to transform your virgin lips into khiladi lips—equipped to kiss ass like any self-respecting successful professional!*

*No guarantee, refunds, or threat calls will be entertained if it doesn't.

# getting that job

'BHAGWAN KE NAAM PE EK JOB DE DE!'

The politics of your job begins not with your first day at work but when you apply for the job. Think of this bit as a premeditated crime; a meticulously planned conspiracy that you unleash on your unsuspecting prospective employer. Somewhat like the Pearl Harbor bombing, but not as disastrous as the movie. Actually the reality of it is you sitting at home in your underwear trying out how different fonts look on your résumé. But let's go with the Pearl Harbor bit so we stay excited.

Getting a job is like you going fishing. You have to con the fish into biting your bait and once it does you reel it in and eat it. When attempting to get a new job, there are two fish you have to catch. One is your to-be boss and the other is the HR person. Each has to be dealt with depending on your current situation.

Here are two scenarios to better explain this:

*a) You apply for a job*
Basically you have a 'beggar' tag on your forehead. You have no bargaining power. You're knocking at their door. They have the upper hand.

*b) You are job-hunted*
They have called you and therefore you can somewhat dictate your package and get the best possible deal.

Now I won't get into how to write a good résumé, for that there are countless other books in the market already. But it would be worthwhile to take a look at the sometimes tragic, sometimes happy journey of a typical résumé.

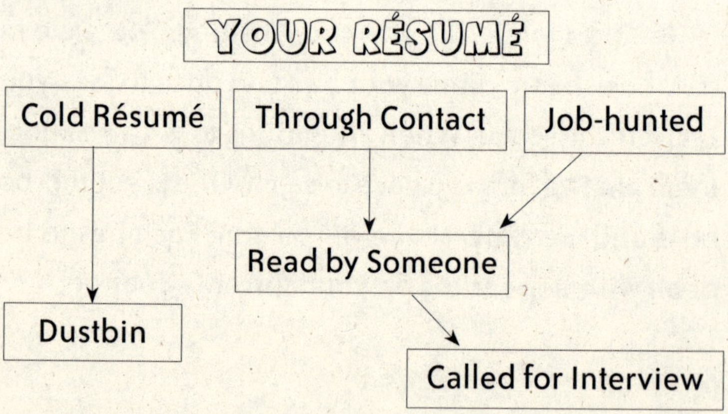

## The Key People Before You Get the Job

These are the first few people you will meet when you apply for a job. Think of them as your target audience. They are the most important asses you will have to kiss in the days prior to landing the new job. If possible, stalk them on FB if only to find out if you have any mutual friends. (Don't add them as yet; that's just creepy and embarrassing if they don't offer you the job.) Check their background and see if you have a common hobby or connection. Try and find something you can casually bring up during your interview.

**1. Your Boss-to-Be**

This is the guy who will be your supervisor. He is looking to find a solution in you. You are what will help him get the job done. So always portray yourself as the solution. Find a key selling point that is uniquely yours and embed that in his mind.

From now on you will be the 'so-and-so man'. It is possible that you may never be the 'so-and-so man' again but it's important you leave him with that picture in mind.

**'So-and-So Man' Must-Haves:**

- A standout achievement
- Simple and easy-to-recall achievement

## CASE STUDY: THE 'SO-AND-SO MAN' INTERVIEW

IPL Team Boss: Hey, you look familiar!

Yuvi: You may have seen me at one of the post-match parties.

IPL Team Boss: Cool. Any key achievements we should know about that will help us decide on you?

Yuvi: Yup, I once scored 6 sixes in an over. Perhaps the only man to do so.

IPL Team Boss: Wow, we'll remember that!

When the boss needs to sell you to the super boss, he will sell you as the **'only guy to score 6 consecutive sixes'**. Congrats, you're hired!

Sometimes, being the so-and-so man is not enough. Here's how you answer stupid interview questions:

**Q. Where do you see yourself five years from now?**

WHY THIS STUPID QUESTION: Even the interviewer doesn't know where the fuck he's going to be tomorrow. He's merely asking this question to fill time and see if you can give an unruffled answer, which would prove that you can actually form words and string them into a sentence.

YOUR ANSWER: Given an opportunity to work here, I would like to use the experience and learning to be a productive member of this organization by taking on more challenging roles.

**Q. Why should we hire you?**

WHY THIS STUPID QUESTION: The interviewer wants to know how badly you want this job. Talk about specific company projects and how you're just dying to add your specific skill to their future projects.

YOUR ANSWER: I admire the work this company has done in the last few years. The [name specific project] was brilliant. I would love to work on the team and add my [insert specific skill] on future projects. There's so much good work available in this company.

**Q. Your boss-to-be is short-tempered and flies off the handle easily. How will you deal with him?**

WHY THIS STUPID QUESTION: The existing boss is someone they can't fire 'coz he's just too darn good or related to the higher ups. They also want to know how enthusiastic you will be in pressure situations.

YOUR ANSWER: I think everyone loses his or her cool sometime or the other. Though I may feel bad at the time, I will remain focused on the project and concentrate on finding a solution. I will also work harder to build a good rapport with my boss.

**Q. Are you willing to work on weekends?**

WHY THIS STUPID QUESTION: Bloody gandu! Obviously the boss doesn't want to come on a weekend and is checking if he can comfortably delegate to you. By saying you will do whatever it takes to complete the job (see answer below) you are not explicitly stating that you will work over the weekend but ensuring him that the job will be done. Hopefully you will have someone to delegate to. ☺

YOUR ANSWER: I will do whatever it takes to complete the job on time.

**Q. What salary are you expecting?**

WHY THIS STUPID QUESTION: The boss wants to ensure you don't make more than him and people on the same level. Do some research on salary paid at your level with your experience.

YOUR ANSWER: My last CTC was 200 crore and I would like a 25 per cent increase, which is in line with the industry standard.

### Kissing Ass Tip: Don't Be a Smartass

At an interview, do not be more brilliant than the guy who is going to hire you. You may well be the next Narayana Murthy but there will be a place and time to show off your iconic leadership skills, dazzling emotional intelligence, and frog-like eyes. The interview is a time for you to present yourself as a 'subordinate' to your boss—his solution—not the guy who will one day usurp his throne and take over his position, BlackBerry, and his wife. Point is, at the interview stage do not be a threat to your to-be boss.

## 2. The HR Guy

Remember the guy who is hiring you, i.e. your to-be boss, has little control over your salary. He will only want to ensure it's way lower than what he is earning.

How the salary thing works is, your to-be boss will be given a budget, which will be given to him by the HR dude. This budget will be based on market rates/ company's rate card/your own previous package. The HR guy's job is to get the cheapest possible person at the lowest possible cost to the company.

Imagine you are a vegetable vendor selling your veggies to a housewife. In this case the housewife is the HR executive and you are selling yourself. Now the thing is you have already sold yourself as a good veggie to your to-be boss—the HR is the middleman who will haggle on the price. Keep smiling and stick to what the current market price is.

Your best bet would be to tell the HR dude that you need 30 per cent more than your current package. He'll play hardball. Not because he hates you or thinks you're not worth it, but because it will help his KRAs and the saved budget will eventually go towards more profit for the company. Depending on the industry and your own cockiness you could even get a 100 per cent hike. This is possible only if you (a) already have a job or (b) have offers from at least two companies.

### Power Points

### Getting a 100-per cent Hike!

Step 1: 30 per cent

While retaining your 'current job' tell the 'interested company' that you may consider the offer if they offer a 30-per cent increase. Do mention that you are very happy with your 'current job', and due for a promotion, pay hike, and a bonus. Even if none of this is true.

### Step 2: 60 per cent

Having received said offer from 'interested company', take your boss into confidence and tell him that you have received a great offer that would take your career to the next level. And they have made you an offer that is quite exciting. If your boss likes you he will agree to match this offer in what is known as a 'retaining amount'.

### Step 3: 100 per cent

Go back to the 'interested company' and tell them your 'current employers' have not only matched the offer but are also throwing in an early bonus and change in designation. Now if the vaastu is just right, this will become an ego issue between both the companies and you could walk away with a 100-per cent hike. You are legend...wait for it...dary! Go get drunk!

PS: When playing the above game, imagine yourself as a high-class prostitute with no scruples or morals whatsoever. It helps.

**FOR THE GIRLS:** If the HR guy is a guy, and you're a cute-ish girl, negotiating a 30-per cent raise will be pretty easy. Just dress cute, be smart, smile a lot, and pretend to be enthusiastic.

Waiting for your offer letter can be a nervous time. Channel this nervous energy by spending more time on FB while at work. Do not ever call a 'prospective employer' or 'add' them on FB/LinkedIn. Keep your interactions with them to the minimum lest they discover what a pain in the ass you really are.

When you do get an offer letter, the first person you should tell is your current immediate boss. Ask him if it's the right thing to do, even if you have already made your decision. This will make him feel all nice and gooey and he'll ensure you have a smooth exit. More on that in the 'Tata Bye Bye' chapter, but for now, congrats—you've landed a job in a different hellhole.

# FAQs

## (F**king Annoying Getting-that-Job Questions)

**Q. I would like to land a dream job. How do I go about it?**

A. Dream jobs were manufactured in the year 1947. The current holders of dream jobs have not yet left their government positions.

**Q. But Mummy says if I get my dream job, I'll be happy, right?**

A. Yes, Rahul, you will.

**Q. Is it okay to lie about skills in my résumé?**

A. Are you applying for a pilot position or a sales position?

**Q. I got a mail from a Nigerian company telling me I won Rs 25 crore, all I have to do is deposit 1 lakh in their bank account. Do I still have to get a job?**

A. Congrats, man! Listen, if you deposit 50K in my bank account I'll give you 20 crore. Deal?

**Q. As a boss, should I employ someone just because they are super hot?**

A. Of course. The work stuff will take care of itself.

congrats, you have a job now!

YOUR SALARY

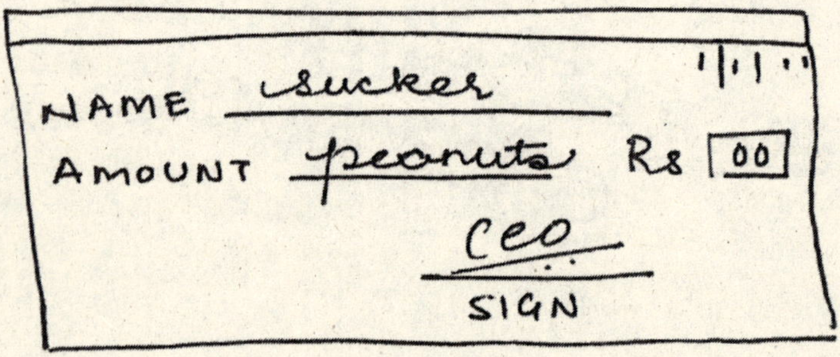

The promise of a new job leads to several fantasies like a better work–life balance, a better boss, less office politics, and hotter employees. Nothing could be further from reality. Nonetheless, the only thing that would have improved is your monthly bank balance. Right? Right?! So here's all you need to know about your pay package and other gross stuff.

## The Small Print of the Offer Letter Now in BIG Print

Once you have nailed the interview and the company finds you suitable enough to take you on board, they will send you an offer letter. Most of us are too bored to read this document and all we want to know is: HOW MUCH AM I GETTING PAID?!

So here's all you wanted to know about the offer letter but were too bored to read. Until now. Don't worry, I'll make it quick.

**1. Gross Emoluments**

The total amount the company will pay you, which will include your Basic Salary, HRA, Transportation, Entertainment, Phone Calls.

WHAT IT BLOODY MEANS: You will get your basic salary every month. This is called the 'cash in hand' which will be personally handed to you in ten-rupee notes at the end of the month while you wait your turn in line in front of the Finance desk. Or, it is transferred to your bank account. This 'basic salary' amount will be ridiculously low for two reasons:

1. This is what you pay income tax on. The lower it is, the lesser the amount you pay to the Government of India.
2. The company will pay the remainder of your money biannually or at the end of the year. This also allows them to hold you to monetary ransom in case things go bad between you and the company.

Other than the 'Basic Salary' you will have to raise bills for the rest, which can be quite a bitch. Basically keep all your petrol, medicine, phone, escort services bills, etc. stuffed away in an old sock. That's your money right there.

**How to Raise Bills**

HRA: If you pay house rent or EMIs, keep these receipts and guard them like your mother's gold. You will need to give copies of these to the company.

~~If you are using this as a means to avoid paying income tax, shame on you. Create a fake rent agreement and make fake receipts wherein you pay rent to your dad or mom. This is considered illegal and so I am going to cancel it thereby making it practically impossible for you to read it.~~

**Sample rent agreement format:**

~~THE AGREEMENT IS MADE IN DUPLICATE BETWEEN ____________________ the Landlord Name~~

~~Address Postal Code Telephone(s)~~

~~—AND—~~

~~the Tenant(s)~~

~~PREMISES 2. THE PARTIES AGREE THAT~~

~~The Landlord will rent to the Tenant and the Tenant will rent from the Landlord the following residential premises:~~

~~Street name and number~~

~~Town or City~~

~~Is the residential premises a mobile home or mobile home space? Yes~~

~~Superintendent or Property Manager (if applicable)~~

~~Name~~

~~Address Postal Code Telephone(s)~~

~~TERM 3. The tenancy is to begin on day of 20 and is to run from~~

~~year to year month to month week to week~~

~~—OR—~~

~~3. The tenancy is for a fixed term and is described in the attached Schedule A which will then become part of this lease.~~

~~RENT 4. The tenant will pay rent at the following rate: per~~

~~Week/Month~~

~~to~~

~~Name and address to whom payments are to be made~~

The first payment of rent is due on the 20th day of the month and thereafter payments are to be made on the 5th day of each month.

The Landlord shall provide a receipt to the Tenant on request.

**Sample rent receipt format:**

**RENT RECEIPT**

Received with thanks from Mr/Ms ______________________

________________________________________

a sum of Rs ______________ (Rupees ______________

________________________________________)

towards rent of my house located at ______________

________________________________________

________________________________________

for the month of ______________________________

________________________________________

Electricity and water charges are not included in the above amount.

(Signature of the landlord)

### 2. Designation

This is going to be on your visiting card and on your future résumé. It will also dictate where you are in the food chain, what company parties you get invited to, and whether you are referred to by your first name, last name, or pet name.

| Designation | Name You Will Be Called |
|---|---|
| CEO | Mr Ambani |
| Manager | Anil |
| Executive | Chodu |

**3. CTC**

Cost to Company. Pretty much the same as gross emoluments, but sounds less gross.

**4. Probation Period**

Like an engagement period. If your boss finds you to be a pain in his ass, he can fire you during this period. Without any consequences to the company.

If your probation period continues forever and ever, you need to get the hint that the company is just not that into you. This would be a good time to get back in touch with headhunters and throw sheep at colleagues on FB, just so they know you are alive, and who knows, they may even know of a possible job vacancy. Not that you're desperately looking or anything.

### 5. Termination Clause

If you have completed the probation period and then the boss finds out you're a pain in the ass, a termination clause will be initiated. This means the relationship is coming to an end and you are in the process of being fired. This is the worst-case scenario.

In order to avoid such a termination, your boss will turn the heat on you in the following ways so that you quit:

- Will give you unreasonable tasks
- Will give you work over weekends
- Will keep you out of the loop
- Will not mark you on mails
- Will not invite you to department meetings
- Will not join you for tea
- Will not call you by your nickname

### 6. Severance

In case the company is downsizing or the business is being 'realigned', a bunch of people are 'laid off' for no apparent fault of theirs. When this happens the company pays guilt money in the form of severance. This allows them to feel good about themselves.

### Kissing Ass Tip

Keep your offer letter in a safe place along with old love letters, expired insurance policies, and bank statements.

**Take a Break**

Too bored to continue reading. Play this game.

**FLAMES**

| ____________________ | ____________________ |
|---|---|
| (your name) | (colleague's name) |

## Welcome to the Corporate Jungle. What Animal Are You?

Hurray! You are an employee now. But what kind? And what does it mean?

As corporations got bigger, and used public money in the form of 'shares', boards of directors resorted to ingenious but legal ways to keep more money for themselves. Paradoxically this could mean hiring you and even paying you money. A company will keep a profitable mix of permanent and temporary employees and consultants constantly juggling in the air in order to avoid union issues, claim tax benefits, and meet legal requirements. It's possible that you are being hired not for your brilliance but to fulfil a headcount. Maybe they didn't even read your résumé. But who cares, you still get paid! And that's all you've got to care about. Depending on what tax loophole your company is playing at, you will be offered a choice of employment options.

### 1. Permanent Employee

If the HR guy is keen for you to take up permanent employment with the company it's because of this behind-the-scene factor:

A new project is on the anvil and after much debate the company head has finally agreed to hire new people instead of doing it with the existing resources. HR and Finance had to come into the picture and sanction a permanent headcount which was then approved by a board of directors. They only approved it because they wanted to move on to better things like discussing their annual bonus.

**Nature of relationship:** Like Husband–Wife

**Typical benefits:** Vacation days, last to get laid off, visiting card!

**Company motive:** Fill headcount, pay structure designed to keep a lot of your money locked with the company

**What sucks:** Income deducted at source

**2. Temporary Employee**

The company has a short-term project coming up and they need someone to do the dirty work. Fortunately the profit they will make from this project allows them the luxury to hire slave employees. When the time comes, and oh it will, they will let you go with no tears or threats from Mamata. Generally you will be treated with minimum respect. This is because most of the respect is reserved for those who are invited to the company town hall.

**Nature of relationship:** The Keep

**Typical benefits:** Higher take home, freelance without guilt

**Company motive:** Easy to fire staff, easy to blame when things go wrong

**What sucks:** No medi-claim, not allowed to stick family photos in cubicle

**3. Consultant**

The company is enjoying immense profits and can now employ the services of a conman consultant, i.e. you. A consultant will spend as little time within the company as possible. Most of the time you spend at the company will be in drinking coffee and in the company of the person who hired you. Your charges are directly proportionate to the level of the person you keep company with. And you can charge by the hour. You won't actually do anything but will consult the rest of the people on how things should get done. And if things don't go according to plan based on this consultation, it's never your fault. Sweet.

A consultant coming into the picture means:

- The MD, erstwhile alumni of one or the other B-school, wants an official reason to drink with his batchmate, i.e. you.
- A department is introduced to a 'consultant', who will give an outsider an unbiased perspective on the company and how it needs to do things.

**Nature of relationship:** Highly Paid Prostitute

**Typical benefits:** No accountability. The only meeting room in the office will be converted into your personal cabin

**Company motive:** Siphon company money into brother-in-law's consultancy firm

**What sucks:** Having to spend time with employees

## FAQs

## (F**king Annoying Congrats-You-Have-a-Job-Now Questions)

**Q. I just found out that people at my level are getting paid more than me.**

A. You just hit-wicketed yourself. Nothing you can do about it but give them angry looks and hope you get a pay hike at the upcoming appraisal.

**Q. After joining I found out that my boss is a bastard and the company sucks. Should I quit?**

A. Stop whining, bitch. Shut the fuck up and enjoy your stay.

**Q. I really hate my new colleagues. Do I have to talk to them?**

A. Only when you want to get work done. Otherwise, stare at your computer all day long. That's why they gave you one.

**Q. Do I have to spend the *whole* fucking day here?**

A. Yes! Wait for the imaginary bell to ring and then run out. But do this only in your head. In reality, maintain your composure and walk out like the hard-working professional you pretend to be.

# FUCK! YOUR FIRST DAY

'MUMMY I AM GOING TO OFFICE!'

Your first day at work will be spent figuring out your boss, your colleagues, office culture, and whether or not there are any fuckable people in the office. In these first few days you will also figure out the least mindfucking way to commute to office, and also how late you can waltz into the office without getting pulled up by your boss. As a thumb rule, arrive at the official time on the first few days. Here are a few things you will have to keep in mind on your first day at work.

Other than the fact that there is no assembly and you don't have to sing 'Jana Gana Mana' (unless you want to), going to office is almost like going to school. Here's proof:

| Office | School |
|---|---|
| Office clothes | Uniform |
| Workstation with chewing gum | Desk with chewing gum |
| Dabba | Dabba |
| Inbox | Calendar |
| Boss in bad mood | Remarks |
| Boss absent | Teacher absent |
| Deadlines | Homework |

## What to Wear

Dressing appropriately on your first day can get you promoted in just three months. No, it can't, moron! But it does set the tone for who you are. You can't walk into office in your ripped jeans and metal T-shirt if you're working in a bank. Well, you could try, and if you do, put it up on YouTube, okay.

As a salaried employee you must follow an unofficial dress code depending on which industry you toil in. Think of yourself as an actor who must dress for the part.

Confused about what to wear? This chart clarifies the dress codes of various industries.

| Industry | Dress Code |
|---|---|
| **Serious** (Production, Marketing, Finance, Consulting) | **For boys:** Dull pinstripes with front pleated trousers. Dark blazers for meetings. Pink shirt if you are confident or Lalit Modi.<br>**For girls:** Woollen suits which subtly accentuate your feminine curves without being overtly sexy. Great for role play if you are newly married. |
| **Super serious** (Doctor, Engineer, Pilot, Bus conductor, Superhero) | In an effort to instil blind faith/ confidence in your customer it is mandatory to wear some kind of uniform. Actual degree is not really mandatory. Again, great for role play if you are newly married. |
| **Politics** (Actor/Gangster/ Lawyer-turned-politician, Son of dynasty family) | Purge all past sins and even future atrocities by wearing a pristine white kurta. |

(*contd*)

| | |
|---|---|
| **Creative** (Politician/Gangster-turned-reality star, Struggling writer, Terrorist-escort/ Model-escort) | **For boys:** Stubble, ill-fitting clothes.<br><br>**For girls:** Silicon, fake designer clothes. |
| **Friday and Weekend Dressing** | Employees whose nature of job falls in the 'Serious' category are allowed to dress up in casual wear. This means wearing 'jeans' pulled up to your navel. |

**For CEOs and Scamtrepreneurs**

Generally bespoke suits from unpronounceable Italian designers. Or use the column below to pick your wardrobe. Keep it stylish, fellows. Image is everything, especially when you are being escorted away by the CBI.

| Type of CEO/ Scamtrepreneur | Dress Code |
|---|---|
| Family-run empire | Raymond |
| Scion of family-run empire | The actress who plays a sport |
| Former commissioners | Ermenegildo Zegna |

| Engineer-turned-entrepreneur | Papa's suit |
|---|---|
| IIM-IIT consultant | Prada's suit |

## We are Proud to Have You (Aka You are Employee Number SR496)

You've just thrown a party for your friends, gotten drunk, and made it to your first day at work. Perhaps you are slightly hungover but try not to show it. And it's okay to not have called your to-be boss to the party you just had. Actually don't even mention the party.

When you walk into office, the first thing you should do is go over and say hi to the guy who hired you. Make small talk; let the conversation revolve around mundane personal stuff—home, movies, food—a conversation that displays your wit and repartee. If you do not have any wit, read out your favourite BB joke.

Talking to your boss immediately sends a message to her that 'you are thankful to her for hiring you' and that 'you are her boy' and she will take you under her wing to bring you up to speed on the new plans and will also introduce you to other important people.

## CASE STUDY: SMALL TALK

You: You live close by?

Boss: Lucknow, actually. In a guarded shrouded secret city within a city...

You: Nice. It's like a stadium?

Boss: Yeah, we have a couple of stadiums in there too.

You: Yeah, everyone should have a couple...

Boss: You're not married, right?

You: Nah, just bowling the maidens over! (cute smile)

Boss: Ha ha! Ha ha! Ha Ha! You are funny as well. Roy, come here. I want you to meet the new boy I hired.

Roy (The Big Boss): Hey, Yuvi, nice to have you on board. Look forward to your contribution to the team.

Yuvi: Sure, sir, I will send ma'am some of my thoughts on switch-hitting. If she

likes my ideas she could forward them to you.
Roy: Great. Gotta go now and deal with Maya.
Yuvi: Cheers.

The last bit is important because you are clearly acknowledging the big boss to be the Supreme Being and you are also subtly affirming that your boss is the first person to know of any bright ideas you may have.

Now, if your boss calls you into a team meeting it's a good idea to take a notebook and pen with you and jot stuff down when she's talking. It will make her feel good—even if you're probably drawing a caricature of her botox-injected face.

If you've actually taken down notes at the meeting, go to your shiny new desk and mail her a job list like this:

*To: Madam*
*Subject: Yuvi's Job List*
*Boss,*
*Putting down your job list as per our chat.*

1. *Wipe smug expression off Dhoni's face*
2. *Win IPL*
3. *Complete all endorsements before next schedule*

*Adding a couple of my ideas:*

1. *Take 6 wickets in 6 consecutive balls*
2. *Take 6 catches in 6 consecutive balls*

*Cheers,*
*Yuvi*

### Kissing Ass Tip: Reverse Pressure

Feed your boss with so much of the stuff you're doing that he/she actually feels like you're really doing work and they'll just want to leave you alone.

## The Organizational Chart AKA Who Sucks Up to Whom

An organizational chart is created to assure fragile egos that they are indeed high up in the hierarchy and to subtly tell lesser employees that not only do they earn less than those above them, but they must also be insulted via a visual representation. The following diagram is supposed to denote official relationships, ranks, reporting structure, and the team. Use this hierarchy pyramid to know where you are in the food chain.

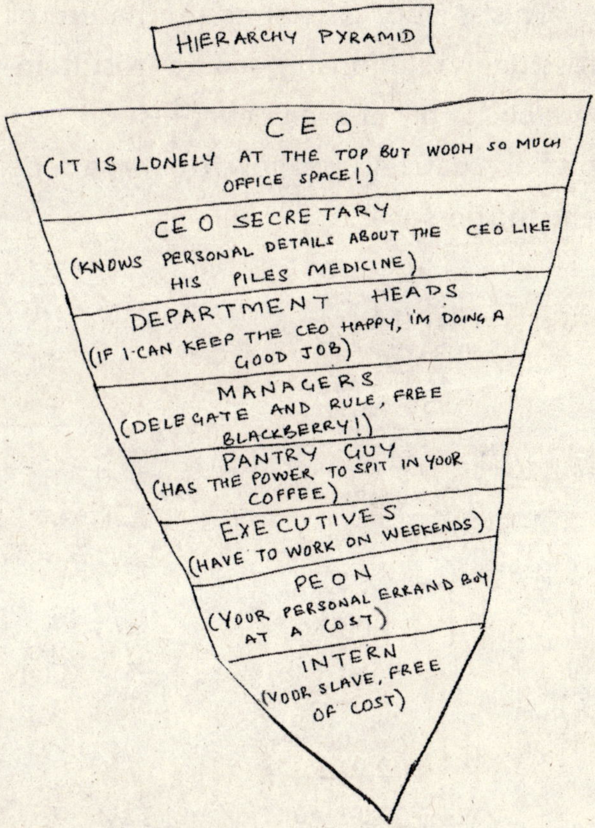


## Who is the New Face in the Office?

The HR guys at my previous company used to send out a 'People Tree' mail introducing the new workforce.

Your company probably has its own funny tradition. The introduction contains the new entrant's name, designation, hobbies (reading, movies, music, etc.), but it never actually tells you how to behave with them. This is very crucial as the nature of your professional relationship could result in your promotion, lay off, or even better—sex!

This flow chart tells you how to behave depending on who the person is.

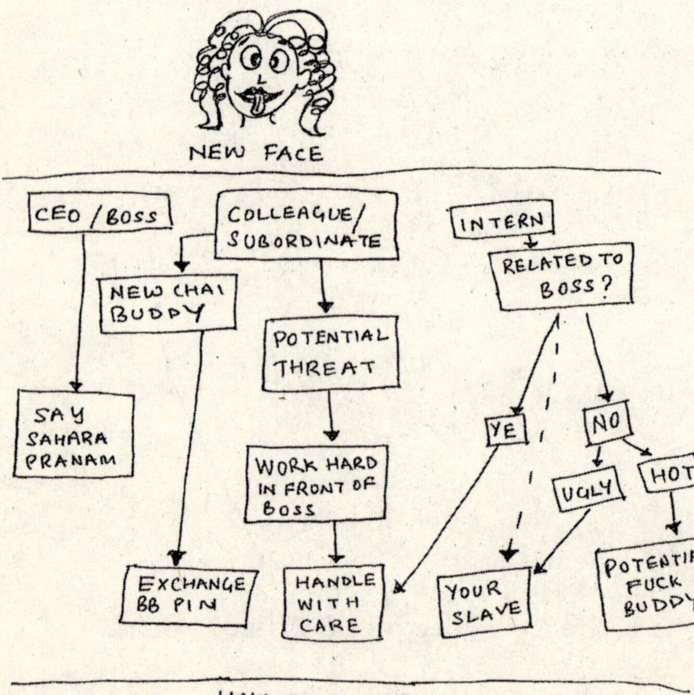


HOW TO BEHAVE

## Lying Aka Introductions, Please

Lying doesn't stop at the interview stage (Wait...you lied? Awesome). HR gives you another chance to portray a false image of yourself in what it creatively calls—The Introduction. Here are a few words that you may use to disguise your *true* self from, er... well, yourself.

| Yourself | Your True Self |
|---|---|
| I love reading books | I read *Playboy* and *Debonair* |
| I listen to music and watch movies | Hobby that takes the least effort |
| I play the guitar | Stored in attic. Promised Mom I'd sell it |
| I love to travel | I go to my native place every year |
| I love to drive | My parents are rich. I don't need this job |
| I love dogs | Below 20. Don't have a girlfriend |
| I love cats | Over 30. Don't have a boyfriend |
| I love to dance | I want to get laid |

## Newcomer Ragging

In your first week at work expect your new colleagues to rag you. Consider this as your orientation ceremony. A way for them to see if you fit into the culture, gauge your personality, and find out whether they want you around enough to work with you. Your best bet would be to play along with them and never lose your cool (unless the ragging is of 'medical college nature'). It's like a playground that you have been let into, and someone has agreed to pay you every month. But the playmates won't let you in so easy. The interview was the easy round. The Newcomer Ragging will truly reveal what you know, whether you have any hobbies or skills at all.

**Typical Ragging Touch Points**

- Your name
- Your clothes
- Your email
- Your lunch
- Your breasts (Acceptable if you're a man. If not, this is not ragging. Call HR.)

Innovative types may also carry out a ragging operation involving the use of office email, a fake project, a department HoD.

This is the test of your confidence and thick-skinnedness. Play along and things will get better, especially if you start the bonding ritual.

## Bonding

Being a newcomer is never easy. Some of your colleagues will see you as a threat, some as a breath of fresh air, others as a devil in disguise, and some may go on to to become your best friends, or even lovers. Bonding with your colleagues should be one of your top priorities. The sooner they accept you, the easier it will be to work and get work done. However, just like in high school, office bonding too has different groups, one different from the other, the nerds and the rockers. To fit in, observe the 'taking break' pattern within your department and then begin the bonding process. Yes, it's exactly like the bonding that happens with your Ikran in *Avatar*. Or like dogs sniffing each other's bums.

These are the kinds of bondings you might come across.

**1. Chai break bonding:** Chai—that essential drink that brings people together. As poetic as it may sound, it's also your key to the office social scene. Taking a chai break or brainstorming (yeah, right) over a cutting is written in the Indian Constitution. All government offices adhere to it with conscientious dedication. So let's divide a 9-hour work shift by order of priority.

Chai = 1 hour
Lunch = 1 hour
FB = 3 hour (intermittent)
Meetings = 2 hour
Work = 2 hour

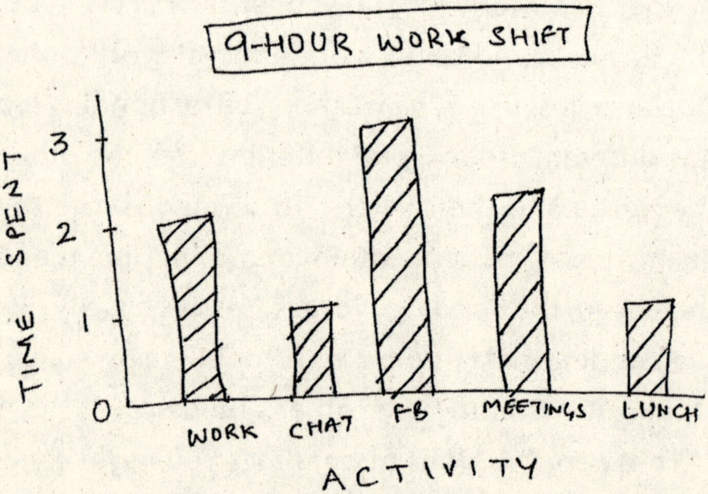

**Note:** In case you are a smoker then deduct one more hour from your 'meeting' or 'work' time as you think appropriate. Go ahead; no one will miss you at your desk. 'Just out for a smoke' is an official phrase that can be used at least ten times a day.

**Cutting chai calculation**

1 cutting = 5 minutes

Ancillary time = 10 minutes (walking, ordering, etc.)

1 cutting session = 15 minutes

No. of sessions in a day = 4

Total time on chai: (15 minutes x 4) = 1 hour

So join colleagues on chai breaks and then at the next break time, ask someone out on a break. Do this with as many people as possible. Going on breaks will give you insights into what's really happening inside the company—the real power centres, how to get work going, and other stuff that's never discussed in a formal meeting.

**2. Joke bonding:** Everyone appreciates a sense of humour, but it's key to know the 'joke culture' within the organization. Do they laugh at 'Santa Banta', 'BB forwards', or 'topical satire'? Pay close attention to the 'in jokes' that only people within the company will get. Make an in joke to truly be considered 'one of the team'.

**3. Smoke bonding:** The easiest way to bond is over a smoke. I'm not saying you need to take to smoking but if you are a smoker you know your work's cut out for you. Smokers find each other in any scenario, and also get along like a house on fire.

There are essentially two types of smokers. The first kind is the one who 'buys' his smokes and the second is the one who 'bums' another smoker's ciggies. A 'bummer' could be anyone in the hierarchy chain. The bummer is a constant cause of mild frustration among the ones who 'buy' their smokes.

Mild frustration because it's uncool to say no to a bummer, because c'mon, man, it's just a smoke. So the bummer is here to stay and he's going to want your expensive Davidoffs. This is a tricky situation that can be studied using a SWOT analysis.

**SWOT Analysis of Bummer Syndrome**

| **Strengths** | **Weaknesses** |
| --- | --- |
| • You have a decent smoke buddy<br>• Great gossip provider given how promiscuous his bumming is<br>• Brownie points if the bummer is an HoD | • Depletes your supply<br>• Expensive charity |
| **Opportunities** | **Threats** |
| • Is inclined to get work done because of the bonhomie created by said bumming<br>• Way to talk to random hot chicks | • You end up giving the bummer two to three packets a month<br>• No smokes left when you really need one |

## Kissing Ass Tip: How to Say No to a Bummer

You can't. But there are other sneaky ways of dealing with it.

1. Buy individual smokes every time you head out for a smoke.
2. Keep a packet of Gold Flake lights for bummers. Davidoff for yourself.
3. Offer the bummer a Gudam Garang. He'll never bum from you again.

*An effective bummer repellant. Since lung cancer.*

**4. Late-night bonding:** Spend some nights working late. This is when people let down their 'professional' masks and reveal their true selves. Chip in on the project, loosen your tie, kick your high heels off, and look reasonably enthusiastic to be working late.

**5. Alcohol bonding:** Join in on the post-office drinking sessions. More on this on a whole Patiala peg dedicated to the topic.

**6. Sex bonding:** Men will be men and will discuss the women in the office. Sorry, women, but you're just too hot to not be talked about. Hot-blooded males: feel free to admire and discuss your taste in women with your colleagues. Girls, you can, of course, discuss cute guys.

**7. Work bonding:** Yes, you can even bond over some actual work! Join the team in the latest project and offer your awesome expertise. Cautionary note: observe the team dynamics so as not to step on anyone's toes.

## Kissing Ass Getting-to-Know-People Checklist

First rule: never go over alone and introduce yourself. The way to meet cool people is to pretend to do some hardcore work. So:

a) Send work-related emails.

b) Get yourself into meetings (just to check out the chicks/guys). Make intelligent remarks. Or stay quiet but interject now and then with a 'brilliant!'.

c) Attend the lameass orientation session that HR has lined up for you.
d) Go for as many chai breaks as possible.

## FAQs

## (F**king Annoying First-Day Questions)

**Q. Should I get a stylish haircut for my new job?**

A. Go ahead, get a haircut, polish your teeth, and shave your ass hair. It's going to go back to square one in a few days anyway. First impressions matter but are totally overrated. You're going to be under the scanner so show up, find out what you have to do, and do it.

**Q. Er, I just reached my desk, who do I talk to first?**

A. Talk to the person sitting next to you. If you don't, your shyness will be misinterpreted for cockiness. Find out what they're doing and play along with their general outlook towards the office without offering any opinions. Ask the boss what exactly you need to do. Or, better still, offer to hop on to a project.

**Q. Take a lunch break or not?**

A. Yes. On your first day maybe you could avoid carrying a dabba from home, allowing you to know what the standard lunch routine is among your colleagues. Never eat alone, not on the first day. Weirdo.

**Q. I noticed my colleagues bitching about the boss. Should I join in?**

A. Better to keep your trap shut for now, but feel free to laugh along so they know you are one of them and not someone who is the boss's mole. Especially if you are.

**Q. It's 6 p.m., can I leave?**

A. Rule of thumb: for the first few weeks leave ten minutes after your boss has left the building. Use this overtime to play Angry Birds or water your vegetables on Farmville.

# YOUR DAY-PRISON

The purpose of an office space is to provide a place for people to engage in constructive activities for the benefit of the company. However, in reality it is more popular as a place to discuss Sachin's innings, check FB, flirt, and eat really bad canteen food (no matter how many times you change the caterer). So, a typical office will be a place where the shit occasionally hits the fan. A not-so-typical office would occasionally also take a hitting by a plane. If you are not a terrorist and want to set up an office, here's what a typical office needs to have:

- Receptionist who wanted to be a model
- Central AC that is always set to make you feel cold
- People walking around purposefully

- People staring at their laptops like their lives depended on it
- One random person in the loo at all times

Study this office map so that you can look cool and confident walking around holding an important-looking file.

**CEO cabin:** The buck stops here. Before stopping everywhere else. This is also where they store the most expensive laptop.

**HoD cabin:** When the occupant leaves, so can you.

**Reception area:** Occupied by a heavily made-up graduate who applied for Miss India but got eliminated in the fourth round. This area is unoccupied exactly after 6 p.m.

**Cubicles:** For the guys who are just waiting to get into a cabin.

**Workstation:** Personal movie library + FB status updating device.

**Loo:** Not a great place to be introduced to the CEO.

**Water cooler:** Interdepartment meeting place.

**Meeting room:** Mankind's time-wasting invention. No one has taken credit for it yet!

**Canteen:** Official time-wasting place. One hour is what it says in the 'official' handbook. But you know better, don't you.

**Recreation room:** A room your boss opens up during appraisal time. You will plead innocent to the charge of spending too much time in it. Lesson: Play X Box at home.

## Office Habitat

The area around the office is your habitat—the raison d'être you go to office. Don't sign the offer letter unless it has the following:

1. Chai tapri: For cutting, gossip, and egg bhurji. With extra chillies.
2. Ciggie shop: Share lights and mingle with fellow smokers. Before a pit stop at aforementioned chai tapri.
3. Cheap bar: For the rare but delightful afternoon drink and inevitable one beer post work.
4. Veg restaurant: Cheap good food. Mostly south Indian.
5. Mall: For long Friday lunches or when you want to catch a movie mid-week.

## Quick Guide to Departments

Offices are divided by departments to denote specific functions done by them. Bitter interdepartment blame games are fought in meeting rooms.

> **Production:** Theoretically, the engine that runs the company; practically, the department that outsources all the real work to labourers.

**Marketing:** MBA types with the best haircuts. They spend the entire budget on ads and aforementioned haircuts.

**Finance:** They release pay cheques and fudge company accounts before audits.

**Sales:** The bastion for the company pimps. Also the cutest girls.

**HR:** They hire and fire you with equal amount of enthusiasm.

## Desktop Decoder

As far as dwelling goes, you spend more time at your office desktops than your home. Like homes, desktops reveal the dweller's personality, interests, and occasionally a piles problem.

### 1. Second home

Some office dwellers convert their workstations into a second home. A cosy little 4x4 square feet of space reclaimed all to themselves. In a quest to feel at home the second-home dweller will use domestic items to mask the fact that the workstation is indeed an office and pretend it is an extension of their house. It has the same result as spraying room freshener to mimic the smell of flowers. Extremely possessive, you will automatically feel like you are trespassing on their sanctum sanitarium.

**Typical desktop:** A shrine of sorts, the workstation is thoughtfully decorated with family photos, holiday souvenirs, Best Mom/Dad mug, smelly seat cushion.

## 2. Eternally absconding

Diametrically opposite to the 'second home' kind, this type is never found at his desk. The workstation is pristine in condition not because the person has a cleanliness OCD but because it has simply never been used.

**Typical desktop:** Empty drawers with keys in them. Computer used by interns to surf and chat under the pretext of working. Cabinets probably encroached by neighbouring dwellers.

## 3. Disaster zone

The workstation looks like it's been hit by a hurricane, washed up by a tsunami, leaving in its wake piles of office stationary, printouts, and three-week-old food. The flustered inhabitant is oblivious to this state of affairs.

**Typical desktop:** Unopened salary slips, phone bills, offer letter (also unopened).

**Note:** The desktop is not your private property. Stop peeing on it to mark your territory. However, feel free to leave biscuit crumbs, coffee stains, and offer letters from other companies in plain view of nosy colleagues.

## FAQs

## (F**king Annoying Your-Day-Prison Questions)

**Q. What should my desktop look like?**

A. Call in sick today and draw the following things:

| (What's on your desk) |
|---|
| (What's in your dustbin)<br>(What's on your softboard) |
| (What's in your drawer) |

# THE COOL GUYS

It's a bit of a nervous time for you, it being your first week and all. You'd want to know who your colleagues are. Who are these bunch of idiots you're forced to work with because you weren't born a Mallya?

Unfortunately the HR orientation will only tell you boring stuff like company philosophy, team leadership, and give you an overview of the departments and their functions. FTS! (Fuck t**t shit!). What you really need to know is who the cool guys are and which ones the chuts. How do you make the most of them and how do you identify them. This chapter's going to talk about the cool people in office. The ones who make the office a worthwhile place.

Let's plot them on a Cool–Uncool graph:

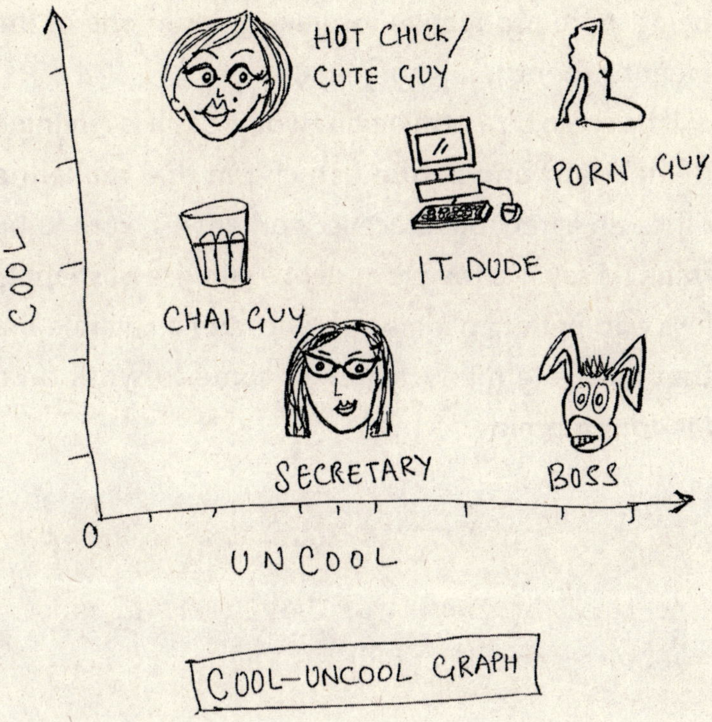


**1. Hot Chicks/Cute Guys**

They are super cool! Having a few good-looking people in the organization is probably an unwritten HR mandate. Good-looking people motivate you to buy new clothes, better deos, and work harder so you can compete with their good looks. Thus the office environment teems with underlying sexuality, and the built-up testosterone and estrogen are spent on being more productive (or having sex in one of the meeting rooms).

If I were to be a gentleman I would say it is feminine demeanour and coquettish charm that make the office an agreeable place to work in. If I were to be frank I'd say it is the promise of a glimpse of shapely legs and perky bosoms ensconced in a Lovable bra that motivate many males to come to work on a Monday morning.

### Kissing Ass Tip

A healthy 'Beautiful–Ugly' ratio in most offices should be kept at 20:80.

## 2. The Chai Guy

Lacing your stomach lining with copious amounts of cutting does wonders to the Indian economy, the tea board, and chai mama, and allows you to discuss movies, the latest FB app, and new job opportunities.

As a hangout, the chai guy and his tapri beat CCD/ Barista/Blue Frog hollow, owing to its excellent service, personalized attention, and stone's throw proximity from your office/day-prison.

The chai guy is integral to this routine and it is necessary that you respectfully call him Anna/Mama/Chacha/Boss/Bhaiyya/Darling whatever tickles his fancy. Now and then give him merchandise (the key word here is 'give', because he needs to know that you are going out of your way to acknowledge that he is a human being and you're being so kind as to keep him in mind when you're doling out charity to the needy).

In the event of his death, do not attend his funeral.

### 3. The IT Guy

Just like your designation, the company will glorify your computer and call it 'your workstation'—whatever! Your computer is your lifeline to endless entertainment—FB, YouTube, movies, and free high-speed surfing. If you don't have any of these, you will be forced to work the whole day! Seriously, quit!

Ergo, a key ally to this gold mine of entertainment is the guy in the IT department. He has a thankless job, thinks everyone looks down on him, and is probably a frustrated software engineer who wanted to join Infosys but has to be content with rebooting your computer. Understandably, he will take great joy in the power he has to block your FB account.

**Ways to get pally with him:**

- Send him forwards of really bad PJs
- Share your stash of music and movies with him
- Ask about the Internet speed in the office. He'll probably say 200 kbps with dedicated ports and a leased line to VSNL. Just nod your head and say, 'Kya speed hai, boss!'
- Add him as a friend on FB
- Give him a lift to the station/metro sometimes

### 4. The Porn King

The Porn King deserves a special note. So figure out who this guy is because he's probably the guy who will give you your stash of weekend 'one-man party' week on week. And just like a girl, all he wants is a little bit of attention. So throw in a corridor conversation now and then, wait in the loo while he finishes his pee. Go over to his desk and talk about today's *Mid-Day* mate/headlines. If you get any kind of merchandise share it with him (the key word is to share, not give it to him because that would be like doling out charity to the needy); he's not needy, he's your peer.

The way to really get him to open up his supply to you is to boast about some porn you got at a vendor and then watch him, like a cockatoo on heat, bare his chest, and run his competition down.

**FOR THE GIRLS**: You may be taking home some porn for 'the man' but don't get too friendly with the Porn King because he's probably mentally scanned you and uploaded your jpeg on chitchatters.net.

## Be Cool

Now that you know the cool set you too have to be cool or they'll run from you as if you were Shiney. As Batman says, 'It's not what you are inside, it's what you do that defines you.' You can still have certain traits that will help you get one rung up the social ladder and closer to being cool. There are many types of functional cool guys, each being cool for their own expertise. You will have to use your discernment and MBA degree to figure this one out. Here are some of the Cool Guy traits.

### 1. Good Food Guy

**Cool traits: Killer dabba, free food!**

The way to someone's acidity is through the stomach. Early man worked and killed mainly for food. Even now, when it finally comes down to it, a full stomach is a happy (somewhat lazy) stomach. If you or your mom can cook, share these delicacies with your vulture-type colleagues. Open your dabba to them and watch them open their hearts to you.

Start owning lunch hour. Your desk becomes a langar and everyone, irrespective of designation, department, and douchebag-ness is welcome to partake of your largesse. Once the feast is over watch them slip into satisfied stupor, soft and agreeable to whatever task you have for them.

### 2. Weekend Planner Guy

**Cool traits: In-depth knowledge about the movies to watch, clubs to go to.**

Who has the time to plan a weekend? Well, maybe you do. But that would be too much work. And we all know how much fun that can be. This is where the in-house, unofficial weekend planner comes into the picture. While outright outsourcing would be considered uncool on your part, the weekend planner is everyone's offline, dependable source on what's cool this weekend. He knows what movies to watch, what club has which DJ playing, even the best sales in the city! He prides himself on this knowledge and if you're lucky, may even have an extra ticket to the hip-hop night at Blue Frog. Boo Ya!

Nobody will say this but this is what makes him cool and is probably his unofficial KRA and the only reason the company keeps him around.

### 3. Sexpert and Love Guru

**Cool traits: Free relationship advice. Probably not the best.**

The go-to person for your relationship problems. The Sexpert will all but reveal the latest in MMS-inspired tantric sex while the Love Guru will listen patiently to the problems in your 'it's complicated' relationship. The Love Guru will have the calm of the Oracle around her and the innate ability to magically postpone deadlines, given your fragile state of mind. There is no guarantee that this person will not share your dirty secrets with everyone in the department. Confess with caution.

**4. Bitch Buddy**

**Cool traits: Matches your enthusiasm and anger in bitching about anyone. Even you!**

Shit inevitably hits the fan sometime or the other. Sooner or later you will be blamed for that shit. In aforesaid circumstances you will want to retreat into some corner and cry yourself to boredom. You will also want to purge your murderous intentions by just bitching the fuck out of your system.

**5. Escape Artist**

**Cool Traits: Houdini-style ability to leave office without being caught.**

Every cool guy who has ever had a work–life balance also knows the art of leaving the office without getting caught by the boss to 'finish that presentation'. This is a skill honed over centuries and all proponents of this trait are part of an elite and secret society called the 'Escape Artists'. They congregate every evening at the bar next to the office. The fun part: You can join them. Drinks on you!

## Power Points
## The 5-Step Escape Artist Modus Operandi

**Step 1 – Perimeter Check:** Do a quick perimeter check of the office layout. If your boss is in prowl mode, itching to delegate, initiate defence process. Get on the phone and talk in officialese. Say stuff like 'turnaround convergence rocks', 'let's negotiate symbiotic efficiency', or 'synergize to maximize'. When your boss goes back to his desk and is buried in his BlackBerry, move to Step 2.

**Step 2 – Avoid Loo Ambush:** If you need to empty your bowels or touch up your hair, first check if the coast is clear. Bump into your boss in the loo and you will surely be dumped with last-minute work. Avoid the loo ambush by going to the loo an hour before exiting.

**Step 3 – Gather Your Stuff:** Imagine in your head that a fire has broken out in the office.

You need to move fast and ensure none of your belongings are left behind. Phone—check, laptop—check, Bag—check, car keys—check, wallet—check, dabba—check. Stay calm. The point is, keep your shit ready and be in to-go mode. Keep the computer on until the last 60 seconds of exit.

Special note: Coming back to retrieve the dabba has seen the downfall of many Escape Artists. See to it that your dabba is washed and packed immediately after lunch.

**Step 4 – Pass Email Booby Trap:** There are always going to be emails. Thank you, BlackBerry. Whatever you do, do not get into an email discussion towards exit time. Leave it for tomorrow's battle or if you must respond, do it over BB only after you are halfway home.

**Step 5 – Stealth Mode:** Get into stealth mode. Keep your bag below your waist and walk in a sideway motion, almost slithering your way towards the exit. Don't stop for corridor conversations. Pace yourself so you don't bump into anyone who may discuss an ongoing project. Choose a path beforehand—one that has no clear line of sight and is closest to the exit. If you have an accomplice, play tag. Cover each other from point to point. Once you reach the exit, don't look back. Even if you hear your name being called. That's it. Keep your heartbeat steady. Stay calm. Keep walking. Congratulations, you've just escaped!

**Word of caution: Don't be labelled a Clock Watcher**

You may work hard and finish your stuff on time, but, given that, for those who work long hours, be careful not to be labelled a Clock Watcher. Vary your leaving time throughout the week. Leave sometimes 10 minutes, 20 minutes and hell, once a month, leave even an hour after official work timings.

## THE COOL GUY MUST HAVES

No matter how uncool you really are, you will need the following:

- **Bag:** For hiding office stationery and that soft toilet roll
- **BlackBerry/iPhone:** For BBM and Angry Birds during meetings
- **Car:** For 'traffucked' excuses to your boss
- **Lance Armstrong Yellow Band:** It was cool. Now it's not. You can't get it off? Get help!

## FAQs

## (F**king Annoying Cool-Guy Questions)

**Q. I'm not understanding any of the jokes.**

A. Go ask Synergy na. Just go up to his cabin, tell him you've felt the granularity of his low-hanging fruits and would like to converge his sheets with yours.

**Q. What?! No really, man, please help!**

A. This is what they call ‘in-jokes’, understood only by those in the know of what’s happening in the company. Pay attention to gossip and study behaviour and attitudes within the company. Sharing an in-joke is essential to you being accepted into the clan.

**Q. Everybody at work has a BlackBerry, should I get one too?**

A. BlackBerrys are like assholes. Everyone has one. So you’re nobody special. Is your current phone cooler than the BB? If not, then yes, play it safe and upgrade. If you’ve got something cooler like an iPhone 5 or the latest Android, stick with it.

**Q. I have a better car than my boss. Is that cool?**

A. Yeah, as cool as peeing on his head. It’s not cool. Underplay it. Don’t talk about it. Now if your car is cooler than the CEO’s car, expect RESPECT from everyone.

**Q. My boss is my neighbour on Farmville. What to do?**

A. First, you're still on Farmville?! WTF. And second, you're screwed!

**Q. Why screwed?**

A. There's nothing worse than boss envy. You can't have a farm that's cooler than his! And he'll know you are spending more time on your pumpkins than your power points. That sucks, man. Move your farm elsewhere. Sell your current plot to your boss. Or gift it to him.

**Q. Thinking of throwing a party at my place. Who should I invite?**

A. Tricky one this. Boss gets a mandatory invite. In any case, she will only show up if:

a) she likes you
b) another person of her designation has confirmed
c) if she has a crush on one of the subordinates

Don't forget to call Pied Piper—he's the cool guy who keeps people together. Get a buy-in from the group magnet. If he's in everyone else will follow.

# THE NOT-SO-COOL GUYS

— SIR, I WILL BE YOUR CHAMCHA

You hated them in school. Now they're at your workplace. See, office is not so different from school after all. You may have asked yourself, why does the office have not-so-cool guys? Can't we just not hire them? Can't somebody just wipe them off the face of the earth? No. They are here to stay only because everyone has a trait that may be considered uncool. And hey, there could be a possibility that you may be one of the 'not-so-cool' guys. Just kidding—of course you're not.

Some guys you may find uncomfortable familiarity with:

**1. Chamcha**

**Survival technique:** Takes boss into confidence and maintains flow of information upwards. As a result boss finds him indispensable. Genius, actually.

**Recognizable Traits:**

- Finds chair closest to the boss at meetings
- Brings birthday cake and cuts pieces for said boss
- Attends boss's birthday party at home, which is only for close family
- Tells boss who's doing who
- Doesn't tell anyone who the boss is doing

**Why he exists:** Everybody has a role to play in life. The chamcha's raison d'être is to be the eyes and ears on the shop floor. He probably goes back a long way and so has earned the 'most trusted' badge.

Even though the chamcha is hated, he feeds the ego of the boss, allowing others to get on with their work without having to do unnecessary bonding with the boss.

### 2. Blue-eyed Boy

**Survival technique:** The boss has a non-sexual crush on him. This could be temporary though.

**Recognizable Traits:**

- Walks with a swagger, even when late for meetings

- Bags the best projects to work on
- Is allowed to take the day off without any guilt

**Why he exists:** The blue-eyed boy is the boss's personal Batman—dark knight who can be called upon using a bat signal or the office phone line. When shit hits the fan, the blue-eyed boy will rise to the occasion, and save the day. And you from doing the actual job.

**3. Rich Fucker**

**Survival technique:** Doesn't need the job. Is only around till dad buys an IPL team.

**Recognizable Traits:**

- Flaunts wealth via phone/car/vacations
- Invites MD for his birthday party
- MD attends his birthday party

**Why he exists:** To burn your ass, only so you can feel his sneering gaze on your poverty-ridden face. Channelize this jealousy into anger, which may just lead you to work hard and play office politics harder. And don't forget to deflate his tyre on the way home.

Worried you might have wound up on the not-so-cool-guy side of the fence? Take this quiz and figure out which one you are.

**Q1. Who fucked up the project?**

a. I did
b. He did
c. You did

**Q2. Whose idea was it?**

a. It was mine
b. It was ours
c. It was yours

**Q3. Do you send mails from your official ID when working over the weekend?**

a. Didn't I cc you?
b. Was too busy working
c. I've told my boss clearly I never work on weekends

**Q4. What weekend plans?**

a. Bidding for IPL team
b. Watching IPL

c. Working again, man!

If you answered any of the above questions, you are not so cool. Cool people don't take quizzes!

## FAQs

## (F**king Annoying Not-So-Cool-Guy Questions)

**Q. I am a chamcha and everyone in the office knows it. They don't call me for chai. I am lonely. Should I stop my chamchagiri?**

A. Nahin, yaar. Who would everyone bitch about then? Aisa mat kar. They are secretly jealous of your proximity to the boss.

**Q. If I am not-so-cool, why don't they just fire me?**

A. Well, somebody has to do some real work. Maybe you're one of those guys.

**Q. Does everyone in the office hate me?**

A. Yes.

**Q. Really, everyone?**

A.

**Q. Hey, are you here?**

A.

(Psst! Hey you, dear cool reader. The best way to avoid not-so-cool guys is to ignore them after getting your work done. At max, restrict your conversation to two minutes. I am whispering because not-so-cool people can't read small fonts.)

# THE CABIN CREW

YOU ARE MY SLAVE!

Now to be fair, these guys are not so bad, but it's their position that makes them bad. They sit inside cabins, purposefully looking at their laptops while fingering their BlackBerrys; a whiteboard on the wall and a couple of industry awards on the mantle.

They are also human beings. This may come as a shock to you, but they also have sexual urges, get stomach upsets, have wives/husbands who fight with them, they also have to pay EMIs, and they are also here just to make a living. Except that they must use you to get their work done. And this is what makes them assholes. Sadly, there's no other way to put it. Anybody who delegates to you is always the bastard. Some day, you will be a bastard. There's nothing for you to do but to accept it gracefully. Let's look at both sides of the table:

## If You are the Cabin Crew

You're top dog and somehow through talent, determination, purpose, or sheer luck you find yourself in the driver's seat. If it's your first day at work it's time for you to talk to the guys who will do your work for you.

**What you should say:**

Hey guys, just wanted to say that I think you guys are doing a great job. I'm not here to change anything. I think the product that you are churning out is fantastic and my job is just to make sure that you keep doing the same thing.

**What you're *actually* saying:**

Hey guys, goddamn it, I'm really happy to have bagged this position. It means more money in the bank, possibly a farmhouse in Alibaug, a brand new car, and a shiny new BlackBerry that I will drool over when I'm alone in the toilet.

My job is to hang on to my job without doing any actual dirty work. That's your job. My job is to maintain my relationship with my boss and make sure our anal sex relationship is hunky-dory.

Since it is my first day, I have to win you over and make you guys like me. I'm actually really nervous that you guys may gang up on me so right now I'm just going to let things be the way they are. But as soon as I figure out the right way to lick my boss's nuts I'm going to make sure you guys dance to my tunes. This means everything will be based on my personal likes and dislikes. So if I got molested in school and was wearing red underwear that day, I have a deep-rooted subconscious hatred for that colour and I am not going to use it for anything. Of course, I'll find objective reasons to not use it. For now though I will smile at all of you and say, 'you guys are doing a fantastic job'.

### Tip for Cabin Crew

Yes, you're human, but when using the office loo, try not to fart when you're peeing. If you're part of a public limited company make sure there is an executive loo, preferably a private toilet.

Let's identify the different types of Cabin Crew using the much-abused organizational chart.

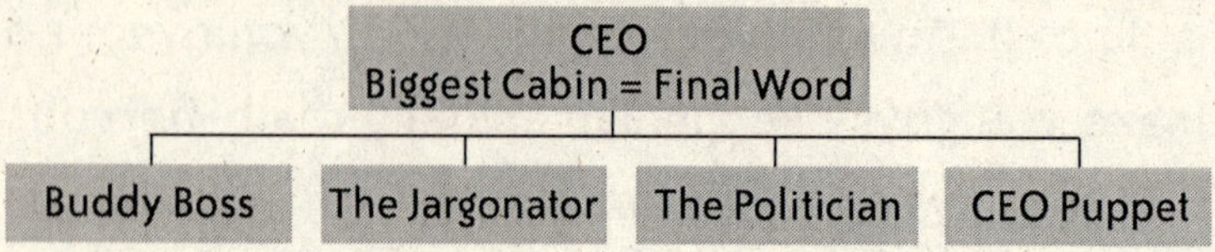


## 1. CEO

He has the final say in everything. No matter how awesome you are, it's best not to rub him the wrong way. Not falling in line with his vision (no matter how crappy it is) will see you falling out of the organization.

## 2. The Buddy Boss

He wants to be perceived as 'cool' and a friend. He'll say stuff like, 'my door is always open'. He'll lunch with you and discuss Uday Chopra's latest debut movie.

Probably the least political, he's best handled by doing your job well and adding him as a neighbour on Farmville.

## 3. The Jargonator

He has an MBA from some obscure university in the States and probably climbed up the ladder due to his connections. He'll have the latest management book in his cabin and will love to use words like 're-engineer', 'silos', 'unpredictably cool', 'convergence' (yes, please add your own).

Arm yourself with jargon and use it liberally at meetings. Be sure to throw his favourite word in. If he's the one who coined it, make it your unofficial team mantra.

### 4. The Politician

The most dangerous of them all. More than the job, his focus is on the political environment and how to gain from it.

Handling him is like having a psycho girlfriend stalker on a good day. Do your job well and stay on your political toes.

### 5. The CEO Puppet

If you look closely enough you'll find strings attached to his hands and legs that go directly to the CEO. He suffers from permanent CEO hypnosis and there's nothing you can do about it. He's definitely the HR head or maybe another department head, and to get through to him always cloak your project/ideas as something that is in line with the CEO's vision.

## TAKE A BREAK

Too bored to continue reading? Play this game.

**Boss drawing: This is what my boss looks like. Yours?**

As Cabin Crew you are a distinguished member of the organization and you need certain accoutrements to create a fortified aura around you. Stuff like this:

| Cabin Crew | Lowly Employees |
| --- | --- |
| Cabin | Workstation |
| Secretary | LOL |
| MacBook Air | Dell laptop |
| Leather chair | Something to sit on |
| BlackBerry Bold | Whatever |
| Office car | Train/Bus/Your own transport |

## The Meaning behind Designations

Ever wondered what the various designations meant and how much power they carried. I'm breaking down the various designations for you. Yes, the wait is over. HR and Cabin Crew need no longer pull their hair out coming up with designations to maintain peace and more importantly hierarchy in their fragile ego organizations. Presenting the designation creator. To be used with caution under the supervision of a certified HR professional. Not to be used under the influence of alcohol.

| Head Honcho Designations | |
|---|---|
| CEO | The tiger at the top. One CEO to rule them all. |
| Executive CEO | Existing CEO threatening to quit? Boost the staid CEO title by simply adding muscular 'Executive'. Throw in a 5 series BMW for some sizzle. |
| Mentor CEO | Appeal to the enlightened CEO with a title that eschews materialistic desires and ego. Ideal for industry stalwarts who are still in the game. |

(*contd*)

| | |
|---|---|
| Chief Mentor | Hey, everybody deserves a promotion. Even enlightened beings. |
| Non-Executive CEO | Ideal designation given to retiring CEOs who can't be thrown out because of their connections. |
| **Power Designations**<br>Meaningless words that add zing to boring designations | |
| Associate | Adds flair to the title of Manager; also stating that the holder of the title is waiting in the wings for his Manager to quit. |
| National | National GM or National Sales Head. An effective promotional title to increase responsibility and feed the ego. |
| Deputy | A title given to the person who will do all the work but get no credit for it. |
| Assistant | A prefix to keep the suffixes happy. |

(*contd*)

| | |
|---|---|
| Senior | Pass it out to those who have done enough time in the organization but do not have enough skill to warrant an actual change in designation. |
| Supervisor | Just a notch above Senior. Given with minor increase in pay but no budget for an actual change in designation. |
| Senior Supervisor | A handy double-barrel prefix to fit the bloating ego when an increment is not enough. |

## If You Aren't the Cabin Crew

You have a workstation and you're the guy who is doing all the work. Well, more than all the actual work it is also your job to be on good terms with the Cabin Crew. Remember that there is nothing objective about a project. There will be crores spent and a whole department that will research on why a certain thing needs to be in a certain way but finally it is the Cabin Crew's personal preference that will rule. Of course, all this will be coated in objective jargon.

The fact is you are fulfilling someone else's dream. Don't fight this truism. Embrace it, and welcome your monthly cheque. Some day, if you're pigheaded enough, somebody will fulfil your dream.

Below are examples of fine dining vs cheap dining:

| Cabin Crew Restaurants | Cheap Restaurants |
|---|---|
| Violet Lounge | Madira Bar |
| Japan House | Midnight Hotel with Permit Room |
| La Poisson de Fille<br>(add your favourite above) | Wine Shop |

## How to Behave with the Cabin Crew

**In meetings**: say at least two sentences. One in favour of what the boss is saying, one against. This way he'll think, 'Hmm, this chut has a mind of his own. I must have him on my side.'

**In the corridor**: quick one-line office talk or corporate gossip. Stuff like 'fantastic campaign, very cutting edge'.

**In the parking lot**: this one's tricky because a cigarette break lasts about five minutes and unless you are the blue-eyed boy, the Cabin Crew does not want to be chatting with you. However, it would be rude for you to not acknowledge his presence. Indulge in small talk. But keep the small talk centred around him. Like:

- Discuss his phone and it's ~~fuck all~~, sorry, cool features
- Ask him about his designer watch
- Discuss the latest item song (if Cabin Crew is male), discuss John Abraham's bum (if Cabin Crew is female)
- Keep him entertained with your opinion on the latest breaking news, India's cricket performance, and the coffee in the office. If you don't have much to talk about just share an MMS clip with him. That's actually the best thing to do.
- If your boss is a woman, you'll never find her alone so just nod along with the conversation that's going on.

# FAQs

# (F**king Annoying Cabin-Crew Questions)

**Q. My peer and I are on the same designation level, i.e. Senior Executive Associate Lead. I've noticed that his cabin is bigger than mine.**

A. A common case of penis envy. There's not much you can do about it. Find solace in the fact that you have a bigger team. No? A bigger car? Nah? A better phone? Nahin? Loser! Pee in a glass and pour it in his cabin when no one's looking.

**Q. I want my cabin glass covered so lesser beings without cabins don't peep in every time they walk by. How do I get it done officially?**

A. You're going to have to avoid this being discussed at the weekly Cabin Crew meeting. Invest some time with the Head of Administration. A couple of beers, smokes, and some merchandise and he'll send one of his boys to do the job.

**Q. I am the last one to be served by the pantry guy. My food is not even warmed nicely when he gets it on the tray.**

A. Are you sure you're not a natural chut? If you piss off the pantry guy he's mostly likely to spit into your meal. Be nice from the bottom up, asshole.

**Q. I am a lowly employee, but the HoD of another department has asked me to do some work for him. Won't my boss get pissed if I do it?**

A. Ah, the corporate equivalent of dancing with your friends' wife. Do it once, it's okay. Let your boss know about it though.

**Q. He's asked me again...**

A. Is this a pattern? Wow, he really likes you. Do you like him? Good. Is he willing to make the effort of separating you from your current boss? It's going to be a fight, so be sure he's up for it. Get HR involved, get something on mail. Or at the least a promise ring.

**Q. I am the boss and two colleagues have had a major fight and want me to sort it out. But I need to catch the 7 p.m. movie.**

A. This is a classic case of Harbhajan vs Sreesanth. A situation wherein grown-up adults take off their professional masks to slap each other in public. The way it was meant to be. Now, if you are the US and like to put your finger in every pie hole, get yourself involved. However, if you want to catch your movie, tell them if they can play together they can sort out their fights together. Which movie btw?

**Q. Need to give the team a motivating speech. I really don't want to...**

A. There is a price to pay for delegation. An induction into the Big Boys Club (BBC) comes with having to mouth words you don't believe in. The ability to deliver these with conviction will earn you your cabin and right to pee in the executive loo. Make it count.

# LOO TALK

SIR, WOULD YOU LIKE TO DELEGATE THAT?

This is where you go to relieve yourself. You know that. And you could be going for number 1 or number 2. If you're going for number 1 it's okay, but if you're going for number 2, it's better your boss or your subordinate doesn't see you. It's just one of those things—we all do it but it's a bit embarrassing to be caught doing it.

So you're in the loo having a pee, whistling away and suddenly the department HoD lines up next to you and unzips, you suddenly freeze! See, he doesn't give a damn who you are but some fake courtesy deigns it necessary to indulge in pee talk with you. This, to me, is the true test of stand-up comedy.

The point is to not leave any dead/blank space in the two minutes. Fill it with a couple of short and sweet lines. Think of these lines as a real life 'Tweet', maybe a 'Pweet'. Something like, 'Salman looks so drunk on Bigg Boss, right?' Or 'If the actress from yesteryears who always wears white does any more surgery they won't need a wax statue of her.'

Your job is to end the punchline just before the boss is wiping his hands and has opened the loo door to walk out. This way both of you will be laughing at a joke while another person walking in will think, 'Wow, that guy is so cool; he made the boss laugh.'

**Focus on these points:**

- He's here to relieve himself
- Don't get into heavy topics such as Q1 results, downsizing plan, etc.
- Relieve him of some stress with a quick one-line joke/a dirty SMS
- A relevant in-office wit (Example: If Shekar puts on any more weight we're going to have to give him a cabin).

Now if your boss does bring up a work-based topic (gandu), then it's best to take it head on but only with bullet-point headlines. Summarize with these three points:

**1. Talk specifics**

YOU: The new iPad is shaping up well; the round design that you suggested is awesome.

**2. Time bound**

YOU: The Indian FB will be ready by end of day.

**3. Approval**

YOU: Whenever you have some time, please take a look at the new flying Nano. It doesn't catch fire.

Just ensure the work-based conversation doesn't go downhill. Don't get into a debate, do not invite a discussion; just skim the surface, give him the trailer, close it, and he'll zip up and leave with a smile on his relieved face.

## FAQs

## (F**king Annoying Loo-Talk Questions)

**Q. I just…well you know…**

A. No problemo. Woh (holds breath). Keep whistling and move over to the basin.

**Q. You don't understand. I'm the CEO and two branch managers heard it. Should I fire them?**

A. I know, it's all over the office. Everyone's talking about it. You've given us something to talk about our entire working life. You're awesome. Don't fire the poor buggers. Just let it be.

**Q. I'm taking a dump and my phone's ringing. Should I answer it?**

A. Why, is it Amitabh Bachchan? Is he calling to help your friend win a crore? No, we don't want to listen to your crap while you crap. Can't you just reread select SMSs like the rest of us.

**Q. Was putting on my lipstick and bitching my boss out when she walked into the loo. How do I switch topics without her finding out?**

A. Remain calm. Keep your hand steady as you continue to apply your lipstick. Then without a beat, bitch about another boss, bringing your boss into the bitch session. Yeah, that's right, get really into it.

**Q. The other boss just walked out of one of the loos.**

A. Oh shit! Abandon lipstick and run.

**Q. Did my job, reached level 5 on Angry Birds, was feeling triumphant till I found out there's no water in the flush?**

A. I don't believe you. Level 5?! Okay okay, let's deal with the matter at hand. Lie low till you can figure there's nobody else in the washroom. Check all belongings. Open the door and leave the crime scene unnoticed.

# email etiquette

This seemingly innocuous activity has been the Achilles heel of many an ambitious Troy. It has done in employees with a single click of the 'Send' button. Beware its powers, for not knowing how to wield the unwritten rules of sending office emails could come at the cost of your promotion, or worse, getting you off on the wrong foot with the Cabin Crew.

If you think sending an email is the simple act of communicating something to someone then you are an innocent acolyte (aka a noob aka a chut). You don't want to be that because remember the messenger always gets killed.

There are many subtexts to sending an email, all of which serve various purposes. The email is a multi-purpose tool-cum-weapon to be used as necessary.

## Email as Sucking-up Tool

Every human being is an inflated walking-talking ego. This ego needs to be constantly inflated by those around him.

Use the subtle email to inflate your boss's ego without actually putting your mouth around his penis (change gender and sexual organ as per requirement).

When sending a mail that is addressed to a motley crew consisting of peers, boss, superiors, and lowly subordinates, follow this pecking order:

*TO: Person meant to receive mail, Peer(s), Lowly subordinates (only if required)*

*cc: Superiors, Immediate Boss, Super Boss (only if required)*

The template is pertinent because it very subtly allows the boss to be the king of the email address bar. By putting his name in the end you are giving him a silent salute, an acknowledgement of his hallowed superior position, paying reverence to his reign.

PS: For best results, avoid the Super Boss as far as possible.

## Key Points Related to Email Etiquette

**1. Be on the inbox radar**

The actual content of the mail is irrelevant. Whatever the job is will get done without the sending of the mail. The real reason for sending the mail is to be on the inbox radar of the boss/bosses. Therefore, it is imperative that you send one 'important looking' mail at least once a week, if not day.

**2. Mail should only be important looking**

This important mail must not actually be important but merely seem important and should ideally be addressed to your peer or a subordinate. Ideally the content should be harmless updates/status of things that are actually under control.

**3. Beware of backfiring mails**

Never send a mail that actually requires any work done or you may just find yourself working over the weekend.

**4. Open-ended emails are a big no no**

Never send a mail that will result in an email group

discussion and flare up into an email war. More on email war later.

**5.** NEVER EVER bring up work to be done by your boss or elicit a reply from your boss in a group mail.

**6.** Always cc your boss when taking an independent decision or making a strong point.

There are a few types of mails that require some elaboration.

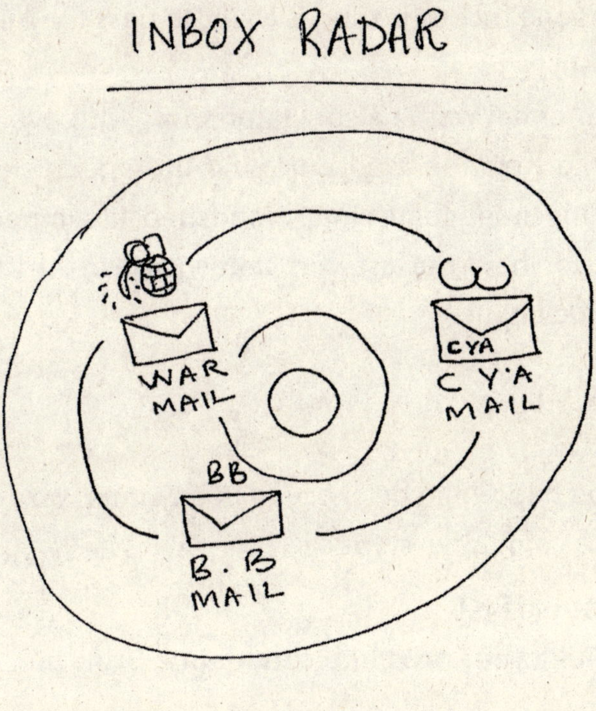

## War Mail

There are times when something that can be amicably sorted by just a chat or a chai, or actually getting the job done flares up into an email war. The reason for this is nothing but political posturing: gaining ground, i.e. a most familiar case of 'my dick is bigger than yours'.

It could be that a peer in your department is trying to outshine you, or someone from another department is trying to gain brownie points, or most likely someone fucked up and is trying to pass the buck on to you.

An email war is a spectator sport with everyone marked on the mail enjoying the spectacle and waiting to see some email bloodshed. It is imperative that you have the last word and engage in the fine art of email jijutsu.

## Email Jijutsu

If you happen to be engaged in an email war, follow these combative steps:

a) Strike first
b) Take your boss into confidence. Bring him up to

speed with the situation and make sure he's on your side. Er, don't do this over email. Go and talk to him in the physical world. #IRL

c) Address your opponent with respect
d) Never abuse on email
e) Stick to the facts and wrap them in long business jargon
f) Use WMDs (Weapons of Mail Destruction): Add bullet points, bold fonts, and italics. Attach older mails, forwards, PowerPoints. Send in a deluge of mail trails.
g) End with 'Hope this suffices' or else use a 'Let's-sort-this-with-the-boss-in-a-meeting' sign off.

## CYA Mail

The Cover-Your-Ass, or CYA mail, is a very important yet overlooked email weapon. It comes into use when the job is not really important but it's important to be documented so that in case it's not done by the 'other party' you can pull up the CYA mail. The CYA email is generally sent to a peer (maybe, a chai buddy) and should therefore be cordial and not intended to screw the recipient but to simply cover your ass if the need arises.

## CASE STUDY: CYA MAIL

Example: Your peer from the design department has agreed to send across the designs by eod. Put this down on mail in the following template:

To: Peer
cc: Boss (only if required and if you don't trust/like the peer)
Subject: Viagra Redesign

Hey,
As discussed, Viagra Logo will be strong looking and the phallus next to it will be erect.
Agreed deadline: eod

Thanks,
(Your name)

## Out-of-Office Mail

In these days of the BlackBerry and smartphones, you're never really 'out of office', so it's okay if you don't use the out-of-office assistant. In case you do, just include the contact details of a peer or subordinate to get in touch with in case required.

Never put your boss's contact number. He does not need and will not appreciate the extra work. And you don't want him doing favours for you because that will only come up during PA time.

## BlackBerry Mail

Love what you do? Even if it screws up your binge drinking weekend? Really, now. Never take BB mails lightly. They are nothing but a test of how quickly you are ready to get out of your boxers and put on your work armour. Always reply to your weekend BB mails with a quick close-ended mail.

In case your boss mails you on a weekend, he has done so only because somebody else is on his case and he merely wants to pass the buck on to you. The only way to deal with this is:

a) Confront the email and see if a solution can be reached at instantly.
b) If not, try and work out a quick fix that could see the actual work being done on Monday.

If all this fails, suggest a solution but leave the ultimate decision in the hands of your boss. This solution should be long-winded and complex. Chances are he will put off the job till Monday.

Ideally reply to your boss's mail with a mail and follow it up with a call so as to close the loop. This helps in two ways:

a) Makes your boss feel important and puts the pressure on him. Ask him for feedback, suggestions, while subtly saying 'at your convenience' aka Monday.
b) Allows you to get on with your weekend binge drinking.

Now, put the BB on silent and go back to doing who you love.

## FAQs

## (F**king Annoying Email-Etiquette Questions)

**Q. Do I always have to put it down on mail?**

A. Yes. Do you want *me* to put it down on mail, telling you to put it down on mail?

**Q. Okay to use SMS type spellings in my email?**

A. Y knot111!!! plz dsyfur dis n req3ssst u 2 reeD n reppply 2 dis widout bursTing ur ey3 ball!

**Q. Dude, check this out, this book that I'm reading totally sucks. What a load of crap!**

A. Huh?

**Q. Oh hey, I was talking about this other book that I wanted to tell my friend about. But your book is like awesome, man.**

A. Sure.

**Q. My friend just accidentally sent a mail to the boss, which had some not-so-great stuff about**

**him in there. What advice can you give me, I mean, my friend?**

A. You, I mean your friend, is a moron and should never use email to say anything bad about anyone. These are best discussed over chai. Tell him that the recall button only recalls mails that are not opened by the recipient. Microsoft is still working on a memory erase feature in Windows 8.

**Q. I have only ever emailed someone in my office. I have never met them. Should I go over and say hi?**

A. Is it someone of the opposite sex? Are you single? Do you want to cheat? Have you Facebooked them? Is the work getting done without the boring hassle of actually talking to them face to face? Don't bother.

# EGO MASSAGE TECHNIQUES

TEAM, I AM READY FOR
MY EGO MASSAGE

You may be led to believe that your organization is as flat as Kangna Ranaut but then you probably think Rakhi Sawant's breasts are real. Don't be fooled.

In ancient times it was simple. The King had to be bowed down to. Hierarchies were communicated and everybody knew their place. Modern day farces like democracy have made it difficult for us to know how to behave. The truth is, egos still exist and they are dying to be massaged.

The right amount of ego massaging can work wonders for your career.

## The Sir Massage

Addressing your boss may seem straightforward enough but it's as straightforward as the IPL bidding process. While it's okay to call him by his name at most times there are certain situations that call for a more, shall we say, respectful salutation. Every organization has their own oft-used terms to refer to the bosses.

1. **Sir/Ma'am:** Can be used casually but the tone and situation makes all the difference. Is paisa vasool when used in a high stress situation or if you are a mid-level employee who has to revert to the MD on an important issue.

2. **Sirji:** Your organization is perceived to be cool and irreverent and therefore the formal Sir is softened by adding a 'ji', which also gives it an air of coolness. In using it you are acknowledging that your boss is the man in charge while still maintaining the so-called culture of the company. To be used in low stress situations when you want to get routine approvals or when you want to apply for chutti. Use it three to four times a week so it doesn't seem odd when you use it for its actual intended purpose.

Example:

*Boss: Pranab, bro, will you be attending the opening ceremony of the Commonwealth Games with me?*

*You: Sirji, had applied and got approval for leave three years ago. Taking the wife on a romantic three-day cruise to Singapore.*

3. **Chief:** A slightly more reverent term generally reserved for the CEO or MD of the company. It also suggests proximity to the CEO and therefore to be used sparingly and/or if you are an HoD reporting in to the CEO.

Example:

*Boss: PC, the opposition is asking for a reply on Bhopal. Do we have our presentation ready?*

*PC: Chief, I sent it to your secretary for your approval a couple of days back. If you think the presentation is okay I'll send it to the media desk.*

4. **Boss Man:** A reverent term equivalent to 'your majesty' and is to be used when men among equals are talking about/to the Supremo. Best used in high-powered HoD meetings or internal conferences. When not in the presence of the boss it's cool to call him names. It helps in the bonding process among the ranks.

Common names used in offices:

a) **Uncle/Aunty:** Not so derogatory, almost endearing. Generally used without much malice. Unless the boss is male and referred to as Aunty.
b) **Chodu:** Not endearing. Used when you are pissed off with the boss. Use it among peers of the same rank and never in front of the boss's chamcha.

## Code Names for the Boss

Most offices have a specific code name for the boss. It's necessary that you know what this name is so you're part of the inner circle. It would be totally awesome if you come up with a code name for the boss. Here are a few ways you could come up with a code name for your boss.

1. **Often used word by boss:** If your boss uses the term 'synergy' every single day, you could call him that.

Example:

Synergy wants us to work on a Sunday and send him the presentation. The Chodu will be at his bungalow in Lavasa.

2. **Name play:** Take your boss's name and put it through your creative Thesaurus. Rhyme it, attach it to brands, desify it for best results.

CODE NAME = BOSS NAME X RHYME

Example:

Your boss's name is Gopal.

Gopal Gas Tragedy (GGT) wants us to redo the design by eod.

## The Chair Massage

When entering into a meeting that involves your boss or 'the boss', reserve a chair for him. If all chairs are taken, offer yours to him. He may, out of false modesty, refuse your offer, but force him, 'Nahin nahin, Sirji, please sit.'

If left standing he is bound to gain the hierarchical high ground by shooting down the group idea/ presentation just to restore his supremacy.

In a meeting room give the centremost chair or the one at the head of the table to the boss. He may not admit it but being the centre of attention aka the 'power centre' will put him in an agreeable disposition.

## The Card Massage

When meeting a client for the first time, accept their visiting card delicately. As if you are holding their newborn baby. Then look at the card for a whole 20 seconds, preening at its design, the finish, and finally the deserving name that accompanies the distinguished designation. After that, keep the card in front of you or ahead of your notebook, where it occupies pride of place, implying to the owner of the card your respect for him and his post.

If the project does not go as desired, use the visiting card as a coaster.

### Take a Break

Too bored to continue reading? Play this game with your colleague.

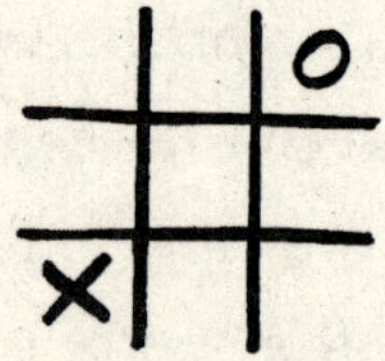

# FAQs

## (F**king Annoying Ego-Massage-Technique Questions)

**Q. Boss really likes the chicken biryani I got for lunch. Should I invite him home or just get some for him tomorrow?**

A. He likes the biryani, not the waiter. Get him a doggy bag tomorrow.

**Q. My boss is an asshole. He never does any work, and I'm supposed to do everything. He takes the credit for all the good work and blames me for everything that goes wrong. How can I get a better boss?**

A. A few options:

a) Dream of the day the aliens invade earth and abduct all bosses to conduct experiments on them.
b) Accept the little-known (until now) fact that all bosses are aliens in disguise, sent down to earth to conduct experiments on you.

**Q. Got a killer forward on BBM. Will sending it to my boss (a) lessen my workload, (b) earn me brownie points or, (c) make him think I'm doing timepass?**

A. a) No, you will be on his radar and get more work. And he'll laugh while giving you this extra work.

b) If it's an office joke, yes he'll appreciate you for keeping him in the loop. Send it before the other BB guys do it.

c) Ration your forwards. Don't send it when he's already on your case about something.

**Q. Is it okay for me to talk to my boss over the weekend?**

A. Totally. Be the first one to call. Or just message that you saw *Dabangg*. It was todu and that he should see it to. He's going to feel loved and won't bother you over the weekend.

**Q. I spend a lot of time in informal chatter with my boss. My colleagues think I'm sucking up to him.**

A. Of course you're sucking up to him. Wear some thick armour to protect from peer backlash. If you go out for tea once with the boss, go out for tea three times with your colleagues.

# PERFORMANCE APPRAISALS AND PERKS

PAISA VASOOL

THE MAN IN
THIS PHOTO FOUGHT
FOR OUR FREEDOM.
NOW, WE WILL GIVE UP
OURS, TO GET AS MANY
NOTES WITH HIS FACE ON IT.
ITS ONLY FAIR.

Key Result Areas (KRAs) and Performance Appraisal (PA): these five words are enough to break many into a sweat and increase blood pressures across the board. The KRAs and PA are tools designed by a company to lend some objectivity into promotions and pay increases or decreases.

The HR guys are the only ones who take this process seriously because their asses are on the line. It's probably the only time they actually do any real work. Let's shed some light on these HR tools.

**Q. Will my salary increase be based on how I fill my KRA form?**

A. No. Let's put it this way: the results are already out, you're just being made to go through the motions so you feel like you had some democratic role to play in it.

**Q. But why?**

A. See, the salary hike is based on:

a) The profit the company has posted
b) Standard industry hike
c) Corrections that may need to be made to your salary #pathetic pay packet in last job

**Q. Will I get a promotion based on my PA form?**

**A.** Will Rakhi ever get married? Your promotion is based on:

a) Your boss's promotion. If he gets promoted, it is possible that he may promote you, while ensuring that you still report to him.
b) Your actual talent, ability, and balls that may have led your boss to actually promote you.
c) Your political skills and hobnobbing with your boss's boss get you promoted to a level where you are now at par with your erstwhile boss.

HR will send out the PA and KRA forms two months before the due date, but you will fill it on the last day of submission when the CEO finally sends a mail to all HoDs that appraisal forms must be given to HR by eod. This will lead to a domino effect wherein all HoDs will tell their respective managers to abandon all work/deadlines and finish off with the appraisals.

## How to Fill Your PA and KRA Forms at the Last Minute

1. Mention a few key projects and achievements that had your boss's blessings.
2. Use jargon like:
   a. Inculcated team spirit via brainstorming
   b. Efficient use of resources
   c. Worked within budgets
   d. Allocated team to various projects
   e. Met deadlines with documentation
   f. Innovated by using new methods
   g. Worked with other departments to foster synergy

**Important points to note:**

1. Always rate yourself reasonably high. Get an average score of 3.8 out of 5.
2. When having a chat with your boss, don't complain; just pretend to be really positive about new projects.

3. Write down a few new ideas and veer the conversation down that road.

## Power Points

### Haraami Ways to Get a Promotion

**Steal Someone Else's Idea**

Haraami Level—Prem C

Success has many fathers and you could be one of them. Take credit for a successful idea or project even if you had nothing to do with it.

**Spread Rumours of Another Job**

Haraami Level—Pran

Sure nobody wants to hire your lazy ass but you can start false rumours about it. Get a friend pretending to be someone from a reputed headhunting agency to call HR or your boss. Make sure he says that the company is looking to hire you for a highly paid respected designation.

**Pretend to Be the CEO's Buddy**

Haraami Level—Gulshan G

No one will mess with you if you share an excellent rapport with the CEO. Now it's possible that you've never actually spoken to the CEO in which case you can Photoshop you and the CEO partying together. Stick these photos on your soft board in plain view of the boss.

**Tell Them You Lost Your Family**

Haraami Level—Shakti K

On the day of the performance appraisal, give your boss the news that you lost your entire family. Start crying and then quickly wipe your snot, look your boss in the eye and say, 'It's okay, I've got a job to do.' Don't bother to explain that your family had entered the wrong train and were later found at the next station.

**For Girls Only**

Got boobs? Flaunt cleavage!

## What to Do if You Don't Get a Well-deserved Pay Hike and/or Promotion

Frankly, there is no such thing as a 'well-deserved pay hike or promotion'. Every no good, kaamchor employee thinks he deserves a pay hike even though he has probably just done his job and gone home at a decent hour every day.

Let's assume you really have worked hard because you have some motivating fire up your ass but you still haven't received a pay hike. The reason could be that your boss himself has not received one and will ensure that you don't get one.

If that is the case, become a pain without actually ticking him off. Make a long list of all the projects you have done, your work experience, and that you'd like to schedule a meeting with HR and the top boss.

If this fails, tell your boss that you have an outside offer and you're pretty much going for it. Even if you're bluffing. As soon as somebody else wants you, your boss will try to be the saviour and hold you back by giving you either a promotion or a pay hike. It's not because he thinks you're worth it. It's because he will have to find someone to do your work or actually go about doing it himself. He will lose a buffer and also, it's an ego thing: no boss wants to lose his subordinate to somebody else.

## The Aftermath of a Performance Appraisal

It's like board exam results; except your mum doesn't distribute sweets. And there's no October reexamination. I'm breaking down what the different types of pay hikes mean, just so you know where you stand.

## Power Points

### Average Pay Hike

**What it means:** Things are moving along the way they are supposed to. The company is keeping up with the rate of inflation in proportion to Pranab Mukherjee's age.

**What to do:** Join colleagues in cribbing about poor pay hike. Go drinking. Come back to work the next day.

### Above Average Pay Hike

**What it means:** You and your company are doing well. Or involved in a brilliant corporate scam.

**What to do:** Invest your money or spend it in ways the IT department can't recover.

### Promotion Without Pay Hike

**What it means:** Your ego is being massaged. Actually you are being fucked over. Company likes you, but not enough to pay you more.

**What to do:** Update your résumé. With your brand new designation.

**No Pay Hike**

**What it means:** Company has found your replacement. Or your company scam is exposed.

**What to do:** Hide fact from colleagues that you were the only one without a pay hike. Crib with bitterness. Drink with resentment. Start looking for a new job.

## Perks

The purpose of perks is to numb employees into temporary contentment with the offer of hard cash or a wooden plaque with a lofty title engraved on it. These help in motivating employees to go above and beyond the call of duty and lay down their lives for the company.

### Perk 1: Employee of the Month

Meant to motivate and foster healthy competition within teammates, the 'Employee of the Month' scheme hones our ass kissing skills and gives rise to jealousy within teammates. Typically, HR sets aside a budget that goes towards this scheme. It is the department head's job to fight with other department heads and ensure this perk goes to his department.

**How This Award is Given Out**

**Step 1: HR Reminder**

Department heads requested to submit candidate for award.

**Step 2: Reminder Delegated**

Department head delegates to managers.

**Step 3: No Activity**

Managers too busy delegating real work to employees to bother about this.

**Step 4: HR Reminder Again**

Department head reminded about impending deadline to select a candidate along with threat that if no name is given the award will either be forfeited or given to another department.

**Step 5: Manager Pulled Up**

Department head pulls up manager for not finding a suitable candidate. Tells manager to drop all real work and find someone.

**Step 6: Manager Decides**

Manager draws up a few names. These will be:

- Someone who does work diligently

- Someone who cribbed and threatened to quit
- Someone who worked three weekends in a row

Manager selects one of the above.

**Step 7: Chutiya of Month Announced**

Via mail or monthly team meeting, the HoD tells everyone how he has personally observed said employee and uses words like 'efficient', 'motivated', 'shining example' to describe why he is a deserving candidate for 'Chutiya of the Month'.

### Perk 2: Chindi Perks

Depending on the nature of your work you should take full advantage of chindi perks, i.e. non-monetary perks. Stuff like:

- **Long lunches:** Enjoy a nice long lunch at the nearby mall.
- **Free merchandise:** Mugs, stationery, paperweights. Why not?
- **Diwali sweets:** Corporate tradition that Cadbury is desperately trying to break into.
- **Birthday bunk:** If you can't bunk outright, leave early. *Or* if you're looking to earn brownie points,

work really late. Keep the birthday balloons on your desk so everyone knows you're working hard *even* on your birthday.

**Perk 3: Work from Home**

This is assumed to be a lot of fun but could end up with you working more than on a normal day at the office.

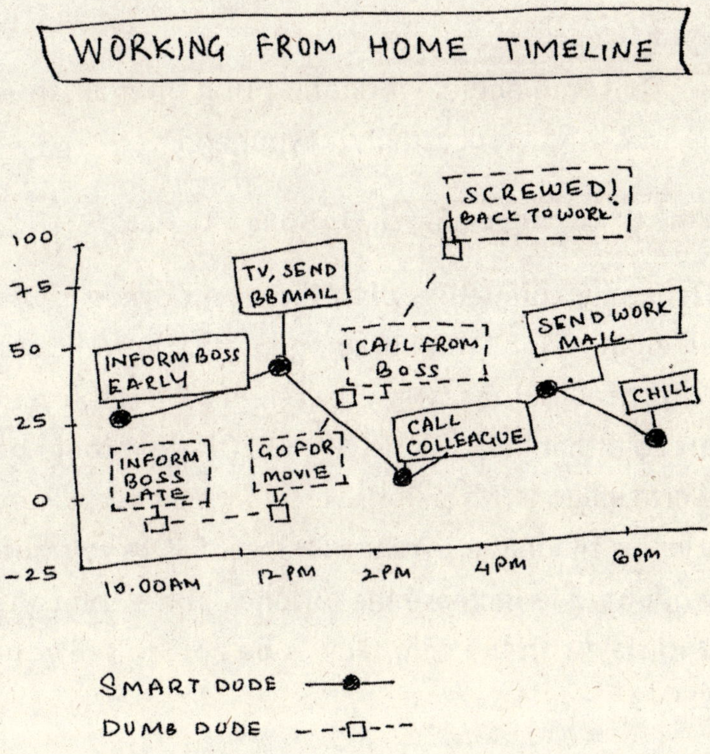

**To enjoy a hassle-free work-from-home day:**

- Choose a day when the work load is light.
- Call your boss first thing in the morning. You want him to know that you're not sleeping. Even though you may be in bed.
- Send mail from BlackBerry regarding something official but not necessarily urgent.
- Make friendly semi-official call to colleague or subordinates to check that everything's on track.
- Do some actual work and put it on mail, thus showing 'work activity' at your end.

**Perk 4: Employee Stock Options aka Raddi**

Generally, companies offer their employees ESOPs when they don't want to compensate you with cold, hard, beautiful, ready-to-use cash. Instead employees are told that they will be given ESOPs that could be worth millions. No zillions. And you, in turn, could be a young zillionaire. In return for these ESOPs you must work hard to increase the fortunes of the company and stay with the company to be able to sell your ESOPs.

**What to do with ESOPs:**

1. Hang on to them if your company is like Infosys.
2. Sell if you're eligible and want cold, hard, beautiful, you know what.
3. Sell to the raddiwala in case you quit before the stipulated lock-in period or if your company is useless.

**Perk 5: Leave Entitlement aka Bunking**

One of the unsung perks of a job is the leave you are entitled to. It's called 'entitled' but that's a bit of a grey area. Some of this leave is necessary, some guilt-free, and some require your grandma to die at least five times a year. Those are the most fun. Your company is forced to offer the following leaves:

| Easy-to-Take Leave | | |
|---|---|---|
| **Type of Leave** | **Days** | **Sorry, I'm on leave** |
| Indian festivals | 14 | On these days you become religious, even secular, all the while keeping your bigoted opinions to yourself. Unless the festival falls on a Sunday. Maa ki aankh! |

(*contd*)

(*contd*)

| Type of Leave | Days | Sorry, I'm on leave |
|---|---|---|
| Sick/ Casual leave | 8 | Wear a jacket one day prior to taking said leave. Cough during meetings. Walk around with a cup of hot water. Monday and Friday leave takers are labelled as bunkers. Avoid, unless your grandma passed away. You will be made to feel guilty about this one. Expect office calls, mails on your BlackBerry and it'll probably be your hardest working day ever. |
| Annual leave | 14 to 20 | Expect to get grief a week leading up to it. Keep in touch with one confidant to know if your position is being replaced. Come back with sweets. Unless you were fired while on leave. |

| Drastic Measures Leave | | |
|---|---|---|
| Marriage leave | 7 | Soon life will be hell at home and at work. Congratulations on behalf of the company. Sorry we couldn't make it to the reception. |
| Maternity leave | 90 | You are now off the hot list. Stay at home. We don't care. We'll bug you with work till your water breaks. |
| Paternity leave | 10 | Yeah, right, you're going to help with the baby. Go on, take some time off; go drinking with the boys while your wife and kid are at your in-laws' place. |
| Condolence leave | 7 | Your grandma really died. And all she left you are her dentures. |
| Unpaid leave | 90 | Either you have found better paying freelance. Or you're depressed. Don't come back soon and you're pretty much fired. |

### FUN HOLIDAY FACT

Did you know that we actually get a shit load of holidays! And yet you complain.

This is how:
(Easy-to-take leave) + ([2 weekends per week × 4 weekends per month] × 12 months)
36 + 96 = 132

**Your leaves = 132 days out of 365 days**

## Long Weekends

The first thing to do when you get back to office after the New Year holiday is to plan your holidays for the coming year. Mark your calendar for holidays that fall on Friday and Monday. Do everything in your control to put out all fires, finish work, or postpone it so nothing comes between you and your long weekend.

## FAQs

## (F**king Annoying Performance-Appraisal-and-Perks Questions)

**Q. I want my company to pick up my phone bills. The thing is I use it to make a lot of personal calls. Like about 90 per cent.**

A. Cloaking one's personal calls as official is the lowest, commonest form of embezzlement. Shame on you! Smarter men have scaled the rocky slopes of Mt. Scam and moved on to charging Rs 5000 for a toilet roll.

**Q. The company is only giving out BlackBerrys to Managers. I'm an Associate Assistant Deputy Manager but I want one.**

A. Hierarchy and budget constraints have slapped you in the face and now it's a nice jealous green. Ha ha! Sorry, you'll just have to buy one for yourself in order to save face. When asked if it's a company phone, just nod allowing them to assume whatever.

**Q. The guy who reports to me is actually quite good. Actually he's better than me. But if I promote him, he'll be on my level.**

A. As a good boss and one who has an eye for talent, it's your moral duty to reward said person with a promotion. As an insecure, inefficient excuse of a human being you must do everything in your power to keep the bugger in his place. At least till you get yourself promoted.

**Q. My boss is a prick. I'm better than him and think I should be promoted.**

A. Keep your colleagues close but your boss closer. Start making your achievements public but always thanking your boss for his guidance and mentorship. Try a combination of taking on more responsibilities and sucking up to your boss.

# SEX AT WORK

things to do:

to do:
Kareena from marketing
Sonam from finance
Salman from Pantry

Throughout human history men and women have not been able to keep their hands and genitals off each other. Chastity belts, religious proscriptions, HR policies are rendered powerless in the face of horniness. Even though the availability of Indian office porn is scarce, sex at work happens. As a force of nature, as something irresistible, as stress diffusing horniness, or as a simple let's-do-it-in-the-conference-room dare. Offices across the world are but rent-free fuck pads that convert from meeting rooms to mating rooms. Having said that, the frisky professional must avoid being caught in compromising situations.

## HR Policy

Fuck that. We just got out of school and college where we were threatened by a combination of moral guilt and expulsion and so we kept it in our pants. Not any more. No matter what HR says, if we see a low hanging fruit we like we should hit on it.

The trick here is to not get in a tangle that could get you fired, or worse an in-office relationship showdown. If your HR policy dictates that employees are only allowed to fuck each other mentally, it's best to keep your relationship a secret. This, of course, would also depend on the official nature of your relationship.

## Starting the Affair

All budding romances go through a step-by-step process but because it's in a workplace you need to go from base to base with care. Obviously your actual time spent on work will be affected as you divert your energies to wooing your love interest.

| Kissing Ass: Flirting Tips | |
|---|---|
| **Do This** | **Don't Do This** |
| Say, 'Nice perfume' | Say, 'Nice ass' |
| Ask her name | Ask her how much |
| Say, 'Let's have chai' | Say, 'Let's have sex' |
| Tell Knock-Knock joke | Tell Knock-Knock joke with your dick hanging out |

### 1. Wooing Stage

Create official excuses to meet:

- **Work late:** on projects and take extra interest in the task at hand. Impress your cute colleague with your brilliance.
- **Schedule meetings:** or find ways for your love interest to be in them.
- **Lunch together:** without making it too obvious. Have lunch but in a group so you guys don't become an 'item'.

Hopefully the above acts will not lead to the sexual harassment stage. But in case they do, here goes.

### 2. Sexual Harassment Stage

- **Back the fuck off:** your advances and attempts to get close to the person are being misread. Get the picture—he/she doesn't like you.
- **No inappropriate touching:** of the arm, or fingers, or any other part of his/her body you have fantasized about. If you are on the receiving end, avoid the person totally. No meetings, no lunches, no nothing. Talk to your boss or a third person before making things official. Not because you are

letting the person off easy, but because it's a better solution.

- **Contact HR:** but this will be long, complicated, and painful. An allegation will not be taken lightly and you will find yourself spending more time with HR than at your work. This is the last-resort stage.
- **Sue company:** and it'll probably mean you will have to work way harder than you would in your normal work, but, hey, if that's what you want to do, go for it.

## CASE STUDY: AFFAIR GONE WRONG AKA KLPD

**Near pantry**

Male Colleague: You are really good on the job.

Female Colleague: Thanks.

Male Colleague: Any other job you're good at *winks*.

Female Colleague: No.

**Outside meeting room**

Male Colleague: So you like being the

woman on top huh!
Female Colleague: Yeah.
Male Colleague: I love a woman on top.
Female Colleague: Good, because I've just been promoted and you report to me now.

**On email**
Male Colleague: I love taking orders from a woman.
Female Colleague: Good, you'll work on Saturday then?
Male Colleague: Awesome, so it'll just be the two of us at work?
Female Colleague: No, you'll be working alone. I'm off to Goa with my boyfriend.

## Keeping the Affair Top Secret

The prospect of a clandestine orgasm between meetings is a great incentive to drag yourself to office. The only KLPD would be your colleagues finding out about it. Then even if you're actually discussing work, they'll assume you are exchanging love notes. Every interaction between you two will come under the scanner. It will be like you're in *Big Boss* with everyone watching you and no confession room to go to! The rules to keep the affair secret are completely opposite to the wooing stage. You will have to:

- Avoid lunching together
- Have no meetings
- Not work late
- Not leave together or come together to work

Basically you'll have to behave like strangers even though you know what colour underwear the other person is wearing.

## Public Display of Affection

Keeping the affair secret doesn't mean you can't enjoy the perks of an office romance. Go ahead and:

- Play footsie under the conference table
- Steal a kiss in the meeting room
- Enjoy a quick caress at the workstation

### Power Points
### The Gender Bias

**Male aka Ladies' Man:** If you're the guy who's scoring with the cute chick, colleagues will treat you with the respect given to someone who owns a fast red car but are envious enough to scratch it when you're not around. You may be expected to watch her back at meetings and the jibes during lunch hour. Keep your best professional face during these times.

**Female aka Easy Lay**: You may be truly in love with the object of your affections, but that won't stop the 'office moral police' from labelling you 'easy'. Wear a thick skin along with your foundation.

## Sex with a Subordinate

Tread carefully because the power dynamics will go for a toss. No longer will you be able to delegate without a tinge of guilt. Objectivity gaya tel lene. Every work reaction whether harsh or kind will be attributed to the relationship.

Setting deadlines will be met with a smirk and you will feel the pressing need to do something about her/his designation and pay. If you are serious about this relationship, it's best one of you finds a job in another organization. If not, then go Clinton on the relationship. Act with nonchalant candour.

## Sex with the Boss

Oh the shame of it all. Your jealous colleagues will mask their envy in ethics and throw the book at you. You will be accused of sleeping your way to the top and chances are that if you continue in the relationship and the job, you will make it to the top. Hey, one looks after one's own. It's only because most of us work in a professional corporate set up that nepotism has such a bad name.

Let's assume that your boss is not the owner of the company. It will behoove (always wanted to use that word) you to finish your work way before the deadline and be super efficient, just so as to compensate for the 'sleeping with the boss' remarks. Life would be tough and if you're not in it to sleep your way to the top, it's best you quit and continue the relationship from the outside. However, you could still enjoy one last quickie in the meeting room.

## How to End an Office Romance

Relationships are complicated without FB adding a drop down for it. What started as a budding romance coupled with the bonus convenience of having the person just a few cubicles away, will now become a painful disadvantage of having the person around all the time. Worse, if you have to work on the same project. Even worse is you can't bitch about the person with a colleague. This is going to take a huge toll on you because you can't just hang out with other colleagues or go for a beer after work. This is the totally mindfuck stage of the office romance and will really test how much work you actually do and if anyone misses you not doing any work at all!

If you're going to end the office romance, do it very far from the office so no one hears you screaming at each other. Take the next day off if you have to. Fine, take two days off. Just bloody stop making your break-up an office event.

## Power Points

### Humping in Office

For that pure adrenalin rush there is nothing better than experiencing or faking an orgasm at work. It's probably the only time you will be excited coming to work. But thanks to 26/11 cameras that have been installed everywhere IT guys can supply voyeur footage to Indian porn sites.

In case you do decide to do it at office, your foreplay should include:

1. Finding a deserted room that is not frequently visited.
2. Searching for and covering any security cameras.
3. Wearing comfortable 'easy to access delicate parts' clothing. Jeggings and button-flys are a total no-no.
4. Keep BB on silent. Vibrator mode is okay, if that's your thing.
5. Don't be gone for too long.
6. Wipe away all evidence. Wear easy-to-remove-stains clothes.
7. Wipe that bloody smirk off your face!

So if you've decided to get into an office romance enjoy it while it lasts because chances are you will either graduate to breaking up, going steady, or getting married. If it's the latter, it's best you don't work in the same organization. Colleagues will have to step around the two of you gingerly. They won't know when you're having a professional argument or bringing a bedroom fight into the boardroom. Also, some of them will fantasize about the two of you naked, having sex. Or maybe it's just me.

## FAQs

## (F**king Annoying Sex-at-Work Questions)

**Q. Was about to step into the conference room and accidentally stumbled on Payal and Rahul making out. It was awesome! Should I pretend that I didn't see them?**

A. Wow, you lucky cow. Playing blind is the best course of action. Without really saying anything extract subtle non-sexual favours from them in exchange for keeping your mouth shut.

**Q. Do I really have to keep my mouth shut?**

A. No way! Embellish what you saw with juicy details about compromised positions, unbuttoned tops, unzipped pants, and flushed faces. These are the little joys you work for.

**Q. My colleague and I are seeing each other. We want to do it on the CEO's table or at least the conference room table. How the hell do I go about it?**

A. Ah, everyone's secret fantasy! Scout the location for a few days. Note timings when most people leave, especially the 'working late' types. Get into a project that will require you and your colleague to work late. On D-Day, wear comfortable easy-to-slip-on-and-off clothes, place a chair behind the meeting room door. Keep alibis like laptop; excel sheets lying around for the 'working hard' effect. Be quick. Clean up after you're done.

**Q. I'm not having sex at work but I'm fantasizing about having sex with a colleague...**

A. Isn't that what people do at meetings anyways?!

**Q. I was doing it but I think the security cameras caught us. Am I going to get fired?**

A. No, you won't. Just don't log on to websites like exbii.com, chitchatters.net, and er...delete that MMS clip I just sent you. It's really not that great. I mean it is but...wanna go for chai?

**Q. The female colleagues at work are really dressing up these days. You know...short skirts, low necks, and stockings. I may have even seen a thong! How do I concentrate?**

A. The brain releases testosterones when the male species has a hard-on. Use this heightened state of being to gaze furtively at your comely colleagues. Leftover testosterone can be used to get pumped up about work.

**Q. Is it okay to masturbate in the office loo?**

A. Research (embarrassing and gross) has found that office masturbation leads to blindness. And, if noisy —unemployment.

# THE OFFSITE

For better or worse we live in a modern world. A world where we are led to believe that we have free will and we have a choice and we have made the choice to work where we work. The bitter truth is that if we were given free will, most of us would go to pot. We would not know what to do with our lives and worse, would not be able to pay for food, alcohol, and cable TV. Reverse it for order of priority. So it is far better that we are led to believe that we have free will, go to work every day, work for a few hours, and get our pay at the end of the month. A necessary evil of this quid pro quo is the offsite or the HR KRA. The offsite is another post-modern tool invented to make employees believe that the company is a cool place to work in.

The offsite is held for various ulterior motives and it's important we understand these and the machinations behind them.

## 1. The Sales Offsite

The sales department motto is 'Bhechch bhenchchod bhechch' and these guys sell their soul and a lot more to make their sales and get their commissions. A sales offsite is held when the sales department has suckered decent buyers to buy whatever they are peddling. They bring in the moolah that results in profits, increased budget, and eventual pay hikes for everyone.

The sales offsite is no cloak-and-dagger routine—it is the real deal. Nobody is dicking around, there is only one agenda—get shitfaced. If you do happen to be on a sales offsite, leave work, targets, quarters way behind and pack only your debauched personality with you.

Chances are the offsite will include the MD, marketing head, sales head, and the HR head. These guys are the superpower centres and the only reason the BBC (Big Boys Club) are around is so the group dynamics can legitimize their immoral activities.

### How to Behave at a Sales Offsite

Don't. Don't behave at all.

Don't talk shop at the offsite, and don't mention sales targets. It's time to make bad jokes, bitch about the VP in the other departments, scoff at how high and mighty the product department is. Bring out the bad dance moves, the hangovers, and get ready to fall off your ass before you get it kicked all over again the next financial year.

### 2. The Brainstorming Offsite

Beware. You will get a mail in your inbox that would read something like this:

*Subject: Leadership Camp*
*No desks, no meeting rooms, no conference room!*
*Find your true leadership personality*
*Let your hair down*
*Chill out in the outdoors*
*Bond with your colleagues*
*All amid scenic hills and lakes*
*In picturesque Kolhad*
*Welcome to the Brainstorming Offsite!*

The real reasons behind a brainstorming offsite are:

- **There is a new boss in town:** A new CEO/MD is in town and he wants to affirm his power (and show off his chicken legs in a pair of Nike shorts). He wants to get rid of all the old ideas and bring in new ones of his own. He needs to cloak this in the form of something official, democratic, and fun.

The offsite is where he will give briefs and you will be asked to come up with ideas around the brief. In the process he will acknowledge ideas that fit into his scheme of things and you will understand how he likes his shit.

- **A storm is coming:** If an offsite is held a month before the new financial year, you've got a real reason to be worried. Here's what has happened. Your company is in deep shit. The Board, the CEO, or someone up there believes that your department or your HoD is not doing a good job. Or the targets have not been met and now it's time for the axe to fall on someone. Time for the offsite dragon to be awakened.

  At this offsite your department head will tell you that you have been hired because you are the best in the business and now it's time to get away from the mundane routine of work and come up with some kickass out-of-the-box ideas. At the end of the offsite, the same guy will tell you that he is disappointed with the ideas and this is totally not done. Ergo—giving him an official reason to sack some of you come April.

## How to Behave at a Brainstorming Offsite

Frankly, you're screwed! There's nothing to do but lie down and enjoy the rape session that will be masked as team bonding. This two-day offsite will be worse than the worst day at work. You will have to wake up at 7 a.m., take part in group sessions, and make presentations. You will be made to go through silly games like 'do you trust your colleague', 'list down five things you like/hate about yourself', etc.

This is done so your department can justify the spends of 'the offsite'. Your day will probably end at 5 p.m. when you will be allowed to go up to your room to freshen up and come back for cocktails and dinner.

There will be enthu cutlets in the group who will take everything super seriously. There will be those who will put in a decent effort. And there will be those who don't give a fuck. It's up to you what you want to do. Best is to keep a poker face, fake it at the brainstorming sessions, and enjoy the 'get drunk party' at the end of the offsite.

What has to happen will happen. You're just a pawn in the eventual checkmate.

## FAQs

## (F**king Annoying Offsite Questions)

**Q. The offsite has been scheduled over the weekend. I don't want to go. Should I call in sick?**

A. Calling in sick for an offsite is considered a grave faux pas. It pisses off people at many levels:

a) Your boss: he has to show team strength during the tele games
b) The HR: they've paid someone else to work hard for this and they know your salary
c) Your colleagues: they'll curse you for having the balls not to show up

**Q. The guys from the sales team went to Paris. Why the fuck are we going to Lonavla?**

A. Because your department is not that important and doesn't make enough money for the company. Now shut up and hop on to your non AC bus.

**Q. Fine, so I'll go to the bloody offsite. Do I wear like normal office clothes?**

A. Nope, fit right in with the rest of the group who will be wearing ill-fitting khakis, track pants, and company T-shirts (mandatory).

**Q. Do I have to answer these personality questions seriously?**

A. Personality test questions are like self-help books —they help the person who has written them to make more money.

**Q. So do I lie?**

A. Lie is a strong word. Let's go with 'act'. Select those qualities that you want to have, even if you don't really have them. People will blindly believe those results—all you have to do is pretend to actually have those qualities.

**Q. But Mr Slick Hair of Conman Consultants tells me there is a leader in all of us; surely this is true?**

A. The effects of brainwashing last for one whole day and are augmented by alcohol.

**Q. Can't wait for the drinking session, but before that there is a boring brainstorming and presentation session. Do I take these seriously?**

A. Take these more seriously than any other presentation you've given. These guys are not some third-party uninterested clients. They are uninterested bosses who have the power to give you more or less money. Pull out all the fricking stops!

**Q. I suck at group games that teach us leadership, team building, and shit. I just want to drink.**

A. Carry your own stash and watch the games take on a whole new level of fun.

**Q. Like what kinda fun, man?**

A. I dunno, maybe your boss will fall and break his head.

**Q. Ha ha, that would be great. But will we still get to drink afterwards?**

A. In the interest of the drinking session, any persons injured at the offsite will be medically treated on site, if not they will be taken off the offsite so as not to inflict guilt on uninjured drinkers.

# OFFICE DRINKING

YOU ARE THE HOTTEST BOSS EVER!
Old Monk
1969
Chenn Chenin Blanc

Drinking is fun. Drinking always leads to loss of inhibitions, sometimes sex, but mostly a hangover. Like a good lubricant keeps the various cogs in a machine running, a good post-shitty-day drink is necessary to keep yourself going. Hierarchies are gone in 60 ml, reporting structures are salted peanuts and soon a subordinate is grinding a masala papad into his boss's argument.

| CASE STUDY: | |
|---|---|
| **No. of Tequilas** | **Typical Drunken Behaviour** |
| 1 | Life is good! |
| 2 | Tell really bad jokes |

(*contd*)

(*contd*)

| No. of Tequilas | Typical Drunken Behaviour |
|---|---|
| 3 | Dance like no one's watching even though they are |
| 4 | Bitch about work and personal life |
| 5 | Call colleague and tell her you love her |
| 7 | Call boss and abuse him |
| 10, who's counting? | Puke on everyone present |

The caveat over here is to still respect structure. A boss is a boss and even though he is slurring, his ego is still his ego. Even then, you do have some leeway. Think of it as a T20 no ball. This is your chance to make the most of a couple of free hits. Just make sure the boss is not the butt of all the jokes because he will take it out on you come sober Monday. Keep the jokes going around the table like a Russian roulette. Pick one harmless colleague or one situation, for example, Tarun's crush on Piggy Chops. Make most of the jokes on the new intern so the boss doesn't feel slighted.

If you are doing some cross-department drinking, sometime in the course of the evening you will have to score a point for your team. It's all in good humour, but it's important you bat when you need to.

Office drinking also filters the Entertainers from the Spectators. They are the storytellers, the PJ Kings, the singers who probably suck at their job but will win the tag of 'team players' or 'good guys to have in the company'. This is also a skill and must not be discounted. The court jesters are the stress busters who are like room fresheners when the shit is hitting the fan.

## Is Getting Drunk Okay?

Yes, hell, yes. Absolutely yes! Getting shitfaced should definitely be an at least one-time experience in your brilliant professional career. The best times to go off the rails are at offsites, launch parties, success parties, or at the IPO party.

If you do plan to get drunk be sure that your drunken activity becomes a bigger hit than the Annual Company Report. Embellish this narration with your own POV, how you felt like making love to the commode. If required explain to your colleagues why you wanted 'Ye kaali kaali zulfein' to be played 400 times. Your colleagues will also know how you cry when you think about your college crush, your Mithun dance moves, and that you wanted an ambulance to take you to the hospital. It's all good.☺

Sooner or later someone else will come along and beat your drunken story, so enjoy your heady moment as the Drunk Knight.

## Working with a Hangover

Vodka goes great with Red Bull but a headache just doesn't go down too well with Excel sheets. Showing up at work with a hangover is life's biggest bitch. And not showing up at work is considered bad form, especially if your colleagues knew you were out drinking. So you have no option but to drag your throbbing head to your desktop and pray you can be under the radar.

## Power Points

## How to Deal with a Hangover at Work

1. **Stay invisible:** Stay at your workstation the whole day, staring at your computer as if you're working on increasing the company profits by 1000 per cent.
2. **Working lunch:** Don't join anyone for lunch or you may have to join in their stupid conversations. Instead say you're having a working lunch.
3. **Don't attend meetings:** Steer clear of any meetings lest you get stuck in them or you are made to think.
4. **Ignore emails:** Leave emails unanswered for the day unless absolutely necessary. Even then, put off the real work for the next day.
5. **Puke discreetly:** If you must throw up, find a loo that is least visited and avoid high traffic hours like post lunch.
6. **Leave early:** Having legally clocked in and registered your presence with your boss, stay out of work's way for the rest

of the day. Make a run for it using the escape artist modus operandi (as seen in the chapter 'The Cool Guys').

## FAQs

## (F**king Annoying Office-Drinking Questions)

**Q. Yeh kaali kaali zulfein, yeh gorey gorey gaal...**

A. Do you have any questions?

**Q. We're going for drinks, who should pay?**

A. It's protocol for the person with the highest salary to make the first move. If on the other hand Mr Fat Pay Cheque is also Mr Kanjoos then allow the one who's the most drunk to pay. Hey, it's his night.

**Q. The drunken guy has passed out and has no credit card. Now what?**

A. The intern pays. Obviously in reverence and in exchange for being amid your esteemed company. And he also gets to drive your puking ass home.

**Q. We've just had our fourth tequila and the boss has started crying. What do we do?**

A. Quick. Take photos, MMS clips; this is going to be legendary. Well, actually only for the moment. If he's a nice boss spare him the embarrassment by crying along with him. If he's an asshole save the MMS clips for future blackmail purposes.

**Q. We're Senior Management, is it okay for us to hang out at the local bar?**

A. It's necessary to mix with the hoi polloi, if only to reiterate the management's egalitarian thinking, provided it's followed by a 'Cabin Crew only' session at an exclusive lounge bar.

**Q. The entire team was out drinking and a lot of us got pissed, including the boss. Is it okay to take the day off?**

A. No way. Here's your chance to shine. Especially if your boss calls in sick. No matter how hungover you are, drag yourself to work. Because:

a) Your boss will feel guilty for taking the day off and won't bug you

b) Since most of you are hung over, it will be a 'no work' day.

**Q. Bloody nonsense, the boss has turned up. Now what?**

A. After a night of letting his hair down, he's going to want to regain control and superiority. Treat him with kid gloves: no singing of last night's songs or reminders of his stupid dance moves. Be all business-y.

**Q. What should I drink and what would that say about me?**

A. What one drinks helps one distinguish between an alcoholic and a connoisseur, a fresher and senior management, a straight person and a gay person. So here it is:

| Hierarchy | Drink |
|---|---|
| Senior Management | Single malt or in worst-case scenarios Indian made foreign liquors |
| Managers | Foreign brands like Bacardi, Absolut, Smirnoff, imported beers |

(*contd*)

| | |
|---|---|
| Assistant Managers | Wannabe brands like Romanov, McDowell's, White Mischief |
| Workaholics and Alcoholics | Old Monk in the afternoons |
| Minions | Local beer |
| Senior Management, Women, and Pussies | Wine, champagne, Breezers |

# *Professional Conduct*

CONFERENCE ROOM

Becoming an employee marks the beginning of acquired conduct and behaviour that is deemed to be professionally acceptable. Depending on the arising situation you are required to be totally fake or employ complicated verbiage that you would otherwise never use outside working hours. Find your own professional persona with the help of these examples.

**1. The Meeting Professional**

As a professional you may spend a good part of your working life locked up in meetings. The way you handle yourself at meetings has a direct bearing on the success of your career. Sometimes meetings are like black holes that consume anything productive. However, they are highly valued especially by the person who is calling for the meeting. Your meeting behaviour is dictated by two crucial factors:

1. Where is the meeting?
2. Who is at the meeting?

| The Meeting Behaviour Predictor | |
|---|---|
| Who's attending | If the meeting has one or more HoDs, it is construed to be a power meeting and everyone must bring to the table their best jargon. |
| Visiting card | Carry a stack of visiting cards and exchange yours for theirs. This bit is called global warming. Lay the cards out in front of you 'left to right' in the following order: 'top designation–peer–hot chick/ guy–inconsequential seat filler'. Make a mental note to say one relevant thing to each one of them. Impress the one you want to do the most. |
| The numbers game | Meetings are also a show of strength. Sometimes what you discuss in a meeting is totally |

*(contd)*

| | |
|---|---|
| | irrelevant and what takes centre stage is the number of people you bring to a meeting. It is believed that the more people you bring to a meeting, the higher the chances of you coming out on top, by the sheer brute force of your number strength. This is successfully practised in the Indian Parliament. |
| Post meeting | If you have attended a meeting outside office, you have earned yourself a nice lunch or some goofing off time. |
| My office | If the meeting is held in your office and features visitors, be sure to welcome them at the door and show them the way out. The distance from the meeting room to the door should be filled with non-work related conversation. |
| Someone else's office | This will depend on the nature of the relationship between the companies. If you are a client you can arrive slightly late and expect to be seated in the best meeting |

(*contd*)

| | |
|---|---|
| | room and offered good coffee and cookies.<br>If you are the client you can postpone the meeting or cut it short to score a point or gain an upper hand. |
| Snacks | The quality of snacks will be directly related to who is attending the meeting. |
| Scheduling a meeting | If it's a real meeting, schedule it in the first half of the day; if it is a 'posturing' meeting, second half, especially if it's outside the office. This way you get a half-day. It's like school. Oh joy oh joy! |
| Taking notes | Whip out your laptop or classy notepad and pretend to take notes while actually doodling like Mark Zuckerberg in *The Social Network*. |
| Take it offline | Ever so often a meeting will get hijacked from its primary topic and move to a discussion not germane to said meeting. When this happens someone will eventually get fed up and enforce the 'let's take it offline' card. |

**2. The Working-over-the-Weekend Professional**

Some weekends there's real work, at others there's pretend work, aka you are there for fuck's sake. It's one of those weekends where the super boss has pulled up your boss and now your boss must show there'll the super boss that she's got everything under control. Therefore, there will be a 'let's work over the weekend' game that will be played.

Expect no real work to happen except for chutiya emails going across between your boss and the team with the super boss marked on it. Dance along like a cheap firang extra in an Akshay Kumar movie. Here's other stuff you could do:

- It is customary to have a relaxed attitude. Spend more time in corridor conversations.
- Casual attire and stubble is acceptable. Even you, girls.
- You can reach work a couple of hours late.
- Although it would be smarter to reach on time, finish off, and leave before lunch. (This would not work in a 'fucks sake' situation.)
- Send a couple of work mails cc-ed to a few people just to let them know you are working.

- If you must stay the entire day, enjoy a good lunch at cost to the company. Force the boss into ordering.

### 3. The Talking-on-the-Phone Professional

Having a phone conversation always makes you look busy even if you're fighting with your girlfriend. Optimize the illusion by putting in phrases like:

- Let's discuss it end of day
- You can't do a turnaround at the last minute
- This is highly unprofessional

#### Kissing Ass Tip: Pace

Always pace up and down while having a phone conversation. It will look like you are negotiating the Kashmir issue with Pakistan.

### 4. The Attending-Company-Town-Hall Professional

Every once in a while the company will organize a company meeting to update the workforce long after they've already heard the updates through the grapevine. These may be held over the weekend and you have to attend. It's the ultimate in kissing ass. Pretend to pay attention. Make full paisa vasool of the drinks and snacks.

### 5. The I-Screwed-Up Professional

Even Sachin has gotten out for a duck. The best of us legends screw up once in a while. Depending on how badly you screwed up, you will have to undergo a redemption ritual to reclaim your former glory.

| Power Points<br>The Redemption Ritual | | |
|---|---|---|
| **Steps** | **Swami** | **You** |
| Screw Up (Alleged) | Sexual romp with Tamil actress. | <Insert your screw up here> |
| Ludicrous Denial | It's a mix of | Wasn't aware/ |

(*contd*)

| | | |
|---|---|---|
| | conspiracy, graphics, and rumour. In fact we're sure the guys at Pixar worked on it. | Didn't get mail/ Isn't the deadline next month?/ It's not my job. |
| Go Legal | An injunction for media to stop playing the video. | Let me get back to you/ Check the mail trail |
| Retribution | 52 days in jail. Now I'm definitely not a man. | Verbal or on-mail apology to boss and if required, colleagues. |

(*contd*)

| | | |
|---|---|---|
| Acceptance | Intend to live a life of spiritual seclusion. Hit me up, bitches! | Finish project before deadline. No delegation for a month. |
| Redemption | Change name and driver. | Change job or bitchy colleague |

**6. The Role-changing Professional**

You were hired to do a certain thing but now you've been asked to do another certain thing. You implore your boss that this is not what you signed up for, but he reverts with a beatific smile that translates into 'I don't give a fuck'.

Professionals are expected to sometimes do things that aren't part of their job profiles. These could sometimes be within the expected realms of official work, other times not so. Case in point: Monica Lewinsky.

**How to be professional about it:**

This is happening because there is nobody else to do this particular job and you were closest and/or the first name that came up in the auto-complete email assistant.

- Think of yourself as an X Men type mercenary with Mystique-like superpowers. Your ability to adapt will be looked upon favourably or forgotten if it is of an illicit nature.
- Carry out the job with enthusiasm; there may be a cute chick/guy that you could meet in this new role.
- Now you can add this role to your résumé, even if you only did it for a day.
- Wear a blue dress.

## 7. The Working-lunch Professional

Resorted to when you have left work for the absolute last minute. This is more of a posturing move on the part of the 'working luncher' to portray a sense of urgency among the hungry clan. A working lunch will mean ordering pizza or digging into each other's dabbas while pretending to work but in reality being totally distracted by who has had how many slices of pizza.

### Kissing Ass Tip

**Colleague's Birthday:**

Polite handshake

Tongue kiss if having an affair

**Colleague's Marriage:**

Attend if cool guy or boss

Skip if having an affair with him/her

**Colleagues Relative Died:**

Attend to network over condolences

**Colleague Died:**

Attend if influential

Skip if designation lower than yours

# FAQs

# (F**king Annoying Professional-Conduct Questions)

**Q. I'm in a screaming match. How do I win it?**

A. A screaming match is free drama for those having a boring day at work. It's your moment in the spotlight. Give it all you've got regardless of who the opponent is.

**Q. The screaming match turned out in a draw. Now I feel stupid about the whole incident. Who should make up first?**

A. Be the bigger man and make the first move. Ask your opponent out for chai. Discuss everything but the incident that just occurred.

**Q. My lunch hour has turned into shopping-for-something-cool hour. Do I message work telling them I'm shopping?**

A. Has anybody missed you yet? No, right? Shopping during work hours is you at your productive best. Just hide the shopping bags at the reception when you enter office.

**Q. I ordered lunch on behalf of my colleagues. Do I pay and collect from them later?**

A. Only if you want to be on every freeloader's 'free food' radar.

**Q. Some guys from work want to car pool with me on the way home. That's good, right?**

A. For the environment—yes. If they are good company, good for you too, otherwise you have to endure their boring conversations while stuck in traffic. Not a great way to unwind.

# THE TATA BYE BYE MAIL

My stuff

Congrats, you've found a new job (aka a job that pays you more)! It's now time for a quickie aka your final blowjob. It's time to say goodbye.

Not too many people pay attention to the farewell mail, but it is important because it's a door that you need to leave open in case you need to come back, a bridge that you should never burn.

If you have decent writing skills you should write your own farewell mail that covers the following:

### 1. Thank Your Boss

Thanking your boss and something in particular about him. His sense of humour, his team bonding skills, or even his Wikipedia-type knowledge of Bimal Roy movies (something non-work related that showcases the well-rounded relationship between the two of you).

**2. Thank HR**

The excellent work environment that has helped you grow, the TT table, and all that other bullshit (this is important so the HR guys feel good and remember you when they move on to other jobs).

**3. Thank Cabin Crew**

A few important people whose names you must take so they also get a quickie and remember you if they are ever in a position to offer you a job.

**4. Thank God**

You just got another job that pays you more for no real reason even though you suck ass at your current job. You should thank god.

**5. Your Contact Details**

Gmail
FB ID
Twitter handle
Mobile number

Or, you can just copy-paste a farewell mail that's available over the Internet. It will sound super formal and obviously copy-pasted but nobody cares and when you're kissing ass they really don't care if you mean it or not.

Whatever you do, do not:

- Copy-paste a romantic poem about saying goodbye to old friends
- Use Times New Roman font in pink (actually go ahead and do that, the world needs a bit of laughter).

If you're leaving because you got sacked or something went sour, then it's best to not write a farewell mail. Go quietly into the night. A farewell mail is meant to make you look good and make the others jealous. If you don't have a new job in hand, just write stuff like you're going to Bangkok to teach English or will be taking a year off to learn *Muay Thai* (kickboxing).

## CASE STUDY:
## SAMPLE TATA BYE BYE MAIL

From: Shashi Tharoor

Dear fellow members of the UPA,

At the outset I'd like to express my gratitude to Madam President Sonia Gandhi and Prime Minister Manmohan Singh for reposing their faith in me. It has been an honour and would be a privilege to serve you again.

The UPA with its modern thinking and transparent governance has allowed me to pursue an unconventional way to develop the State of Kerala.

During my sabbatical, Sunanda and I will be tending young saplings in my native town of Kottayam and I will also be working on my next book 'The Politics of Twitter in Indian Politics'.

Keep in touch: twitter.com/ShashiTharoor

tharoor.in

Forever Kerala, India, The UN

If all this bores you to death, or if you find out you are Mukesh Ambani's illegitimate child, then sign off in style, with the words 'Maa chuda main chalaa!'

## FAQs

## (F**king Annoying Tata-Tata-Bye-Bye-Mail Questions)

**Q. I quit. Can I take some office stuff along with me?**

A. What do you have in mind?

**Q. I was thinking...stationery, blank DVDs, marker pens...**

A. Sure, go ahead, help yourself; that stuff is anyway written off as pilferable.

**Q. How about petty cash that is still lying with me?**

A. Well, that is legally wrong, and could morally eat away at your soul, but from a quid pro quo point of view, if the company does owe you money then... You're not listening, are you?

**Q. I was also cooking the books and have embezzled corporate funds rerouting them to my Swiss Bank account.**

A. You genius.

**Q. I won an award for my team. Can I take that with me?**

A. Don't be silly now.

**Q. Everyone's asking me for a farewell treat. Shouldn't the company be throwing me one?**

A. Obviously you're not high enough and your designation does not approve of a 'farewell budget'.

**Q. So should I throw a farewell party?**

A. How much is that petty cash again?

# Bonus: Just Thinking Aloud

## Real Office vs Fantasy Office

Imagine there's no country,
No religion too,
Imagine all the people,
Living life in peace.

If John could, what stops us from dreaming about stuff that would never ever ever come true? What if there were Funstations instead of Workstations, Bar rooms instead of Pantry rooms. Here's an imaginary awesome wishlist of what a fantasy office would have. HR, are you listening?

| Meeting Room vs Sex Room | |
|---|---|
| • 10 million cups of bad coffee, tea consumed<br>• 1 billion Power Points presented | • 10 billion sperms released<br>• 100 undressed bodies presented |

(*contd*)

| | |
|---|---|
| • 1 billion yawns suppressed<br>• Attendees fake interest<br>• Deals closed | • 1 billion moans suppressed<br>• Attendees fake orgasms<br>• Relations consummated |

| Workstation vs Funstation | |
|---|---|
| • 1 trillion mails sent<br>• 20,009 desk phone calls unanswered<br>• 100 fights for the best chair<br>• Drawers filled with unfinished project folders<br>• Keyboard smeared with coffee stains | • 1 trillion songs stored<br>• 20,010 personal calls made<br>• 100 massages received on custom-made massage chairs<br>• Drawers filled with unfinished video games<br>• PSP controller smeared with beer stains |

| Pantry vs Bar Room | |
|---|---|
| • Lunch hour<br>• Water on tap<br>• Bad canteen food<br>• Empty refrigerator<br>• Rude pantry guys | • Alcohol hour<br>• Beer on tap<br>• Bad hangovers<br>• Refrigerator stocked with booze<br>• Sexy Russian bartenders |

| Office Resources vs Fantasy Office Resources | |
|---|---|
| • Xerox machine<br>• Printing station<br>• Fax machines<br>• Projector<br>• Peons | • Free ATMs<br>• WiFi station<br>• Free web chat machines<br>• Movie viewing room<br>• Butlers |

**Jargonator™**
**A Ready-to-Use Jargon Guide**

| Jargon | Literal Meaning | Official Meaning | Real Meaning |
|---|---|---|---|
| **Get oriented** | Know your directions. East is to the left of south... | Know more about the job. | Find out what your job is and go bloody do it |
| **Dotted line reporting** | A line with dots leading to two paths | Reporting to two bosses | You have two wives. It's a fucked situation for you till management sorts the mess out. |

*(contd)*

| Jargon | Literal Meaning | Official Meaning | Real Meaning |
|---|---|---|---|
| **What's on your plate?** | Food, veggies. Is that spicy? | What's your current job list? | I don't see you doing enough work. I want to give you more work. |
| **Running late** | I don't know how it happened but time is moving faster than me. | Will not be arriving on time to work. | Overslept/ Lazy/Early morning sex and therefore will be late to work. |
| **Eod** | The day will end. No more days after this. | End of day | Accepted official excuse to postpone work indefinitely. |
| **Low hanging fruits** | Juicy fruits that dangle, hang like… | Easily achiev-able | Let's not work too hard and just go for the easy-to-get targets |

(*contd*)

| Jargon | Literal Meaning | Official Meaning | Real Meaning |
|---|---|---|---|
| **Think blue sky** | Is it azure, cyan, or cerulean? | I want an out-of-the-box idea. I want you to think more. | Give me a wild idea so I can shoot it down and bring you back to earth |
| **Bad example** | An example so bad it should be punished and made an example of | This idea sucks but here it is… | At least I gave an idea, thereby setting an example, bad as it may be |
| **Mail trail** | Like throwing cookies to find one's way back | Keeping track of all mails that have been exchanged from the time of argument to beginning of the first mail | A handy weapon to tire an opponent into submission. Used when shit has hit the fan. |

(*contd*)

| Jargon | Literal Meaning | Official Meaning | Real Meaning |
|---|---|---|---|
| **Shit has hit the fan** | Anti-gravity tatti | First signs of a blame game | Start looking for that mail trail |
| **Thinking aloud** | Thoughts escaping brain in audible fashion | Saying what I'm thinking | Should really keep my thoughts to myself |
| **Revert back** | Grammatically incorrect | I'll get back to you, I'll get back to you | Please please get back to me |
| **ASAP** | A small sap | As soon as possible | Whenever |
| **Front foot** | A foot that is in front of the other one | To work with aggressively | Boss not happy with your work |
| **Business plan** | How company can make more money | How owner can make more money | How management can make more money |

(*contd*)

| Jargon | Literal Meaning | Official Meaning | Real Meaning |
|---|---|---|---|
| **Quarter** | 250 ml of rum | Year divided into four months | Time for managers to make presentations to HoD regarding status of targets |
| **H1, H2** | US visa-type thing | Half year | Time for HoDs to make presentation to CEO |
| **Bandwidth** | Radio frequency | Time and resources to carry out a job | Excuse given when you don't want to do something. Using said excuse will return to haunt you during performance appraisal. |

(*contd*)

| Jargon | Literal Meaning | Official Meaning | Real Meaning |
|---|---|---|---|
| **Con call** | Thieves calling each other | A phone conversation with two or more people | Ploy used by con call arranger to signal he's in charge. Other than that a drill for men on how to 'pretend listen'. |
| **Blame game** | A game we never played as kids | A game we will often play at work | No winners. But try not to be a sore loser |
| **Down-time** | Need to take off to spend time with genitals | Need to take off to spend time with genitals | Need to take off to spend time with genitals |

(*contd*)

| Jargon | Literal Meaning | Official Meaning | Real Meaning |
|---|---|---|---|
| **Cost–benefit analysis** | An accountant's version of psychoanalysis | Expensive project requiring thought and research | Price thoda kum karo na! |
| **Masturbate** | Hobby/Art form | Discuss something endlessly without taking any action | Done in cases of a project that no one really wants to start |

# EPILOGUE
# AKA ME KISSING YOUR ASS

How has this book been useful to you?

a) Cheap gift for colleague
b) Cheap gift for your employees
c) Deductible tax expense for office library
d) Bought to camouflage erotic novel purchase

Finally, Dear Reader,

Thank you for reading this book. Hope you liked it. In case you didn't, I'd like you to know there were others involved in this book seeing the light of day. Do reserve some abuse for them as well.

# THIS IS A CERTIFIED SCAM-TAINTED BOOK!

In keeping with the best of Indian corporate traditions, I am pleased to announce that the book you are holding in your manicured hands includes a scam! You may have noticed that the previous five pages are blank. Since I hate probes of any kind, I'm going to divulge the details.

The book had to have a certain heft/bulk, so that you, my dear reader, may know its value, not only by its content but also by its weight. Since I was too lazy to write anymore I decided to insert a few blank pages that would solve the purpose. This way:

1. I didn't have to write anything more.
2. My publisher didn't have to print anything more.
3. You don't have to read anything more but still feel like you have got value for money.

In corporate lingo this is called a WIN-WIN situation.

PS: I know it's lame but so are you.

PPS: If you care, you can use the blank pages to jot down your own devious methods of playing office politics, or you can use them to write down abuses to your bosses. Whichever you think is more fun.

The End

Aka Get Back to Work, Asshole!

# ACKNOWLEDGEMENTS

I've got to thank these people or they will not give me food.

Random House India and especially Milee Ashwarya for being supercool to work with.

The entire D'Souza and Monteiro family. Nigel, who lets me pakao him. Rhea for being there. Chris, my worst best friend, who will never read this book but at whose place I wrote it. Sylvia, Augy, Amanda, Stacia, Aaron for their love and care.

Candy and Marcello for keeping me sane; Shania and Faith for keeping me insane.

My Dad, for taking care and putting up with me.

# A NOTE ON THE AUTHOR

Clyde D'Souza has produced TV shows, written scripts, created annoying caller tunes, and bastardized content for clients. He has kissed ass at media companies like JAM, MTV and 9X Media. He lives in Mumbai and is currently stuck in traffic.